Reliability Aspect of Cloud Computing Environment

Vikas Kumar · R. Vidhyalakshmi

Reliability Aspect of Cloud Computing Environment

Springer

Vikas Kumar
School of Business Studies
Sharda University
Greater Noida, Uttar Pradesh, India

R. Vidhyalakshmi
Army Institute of Management & Technology
Greater Noida, Uttar Pradesh, India

ISBN 978-981-13-3022-3 ISBN 978-981-13-3023-0 (eBook)
https://doi.org/10.1007/978-981-13-3023-0

Library of Congress Control Number: 2018958932

This Springer imprint is published by the registered company Springer Nature Singapore Pte Ltd.
The registered company address is: 152 Beach Road, #21-01/04 Gateway East, Singapore 189721, Singapore

Preface

Cloud computing is one of the most promising technologies of the twenty-first century. It has brought a sweeping change in the implementation of information and communication technology (ICT) operations by offering computing solutions as a service. John McCarthy's idea of computation being provided as utility has been brought into practicality through cloud computing paradigm. All resources of computing such as storage, server, network, processor capacity, software development platform, and software applications are delivered as services over the Internet. Low start-up cost, anytime remote access of services, shifting of IT-related overheads to cloud service providers, pay-per-use model, conversion of capEx to opEx, auto-scalability to meet demand spikes, multiple platforms, device portability, etc., are some of the various factors that inspire organization of all sizes to adopt cloud computing. Cloud technologies are now generating massive revenues for technology vendors and cloud service providers; still, there are many years of strong growth ahead. According to the RightScale's State of the Cloud Survey (2018), 38% of enterprises are prioritizing the public cloud implementations. On the other hand, IDC had predicted that worldwide spending on public cloud services is expected to double from almost \$70 billion in 2015 to over \$141 billion in 2019. An average company uses about 1,427 cloud-based services ranging from Facebook to Dropbox (Skyhigh Networks, 2017). Correspondingly, a large number of organizations are migrating to the cloud-based infrastructure and services. A growing number of cloud applications, cloud deployments, and cloud vendors are a good example of this. However, this has put up a challenging need for the more reliable and sustainable cloud computing models and applications.

A large number of enterprises have a multi-cloud strategy, as the enterprises are finding it difficult to satisfy all their needs from a single cloud vendor. The reliability of the cloud services plays the most important role in the selection of cloud vendors. If we consider the available literature, privacy and security have been given ample attention by researchers; contrary to this, the present book focuses on the reliability aspect of cloud computing services in particular. The responsibility of ensuring the reliability of services varies with the type of cloud service model and deployment chosen by customers. In terms of service models, IaaS customers have maximum control on cloud service utilization, SaaS customers have no or least control on application services, while the customers and providers share equal responsibility in PaaS service model. Likewise, private cloud deployments are in complete control of customers, public cloud deployments are in control of service providers, whereas in hybrid deployments, customers and providers share their responsibility. High adoption trends of cloud (particularly SaaS), inherent business continuity risks in cloud adoption, the majority of SaaS deployment being done using public clouds, and existing research gap in terms of reliability are the prime reasons for identifying the reliability of cloud computing environment as the subject area of this publication.

Traditional software reliability models cannot be used for cloud reliability evaluation due to the changes in the development architecture and delivery designs. Customer–vendor relationship mostly comes to a close with traditional software installations, whereas it starts with SaaS subscription. The reliability of cloud services is normally presented in terms of percentage such as 99.9% or 99.99%. These percentage values are converted to downtime and uptime information (per month or per year). This type of reliability measurement provides confidence only in the service availability feature and may not talk about all the quality attributes of the product. Both the qualitative and quantitative approaches to cloud reliability have been taken up with a comprehensive review of the reliability models suitable for different services and deployments. The reliability evaluation models will help customers to identify different cloud products, suitable to the business needs, and will also help developers to gather customer expectations. Most importantly, it will help the vendors to improve their service and support.

Greater Noida, India

Vikas Kumar
R. Vidhyalakshmi

Contents

About the Authors

Dr. Vikas Kumar received his M.Sc. in electronics from Kurukshetra University, Haryana, India, followed by M.Sc. in computer science and Ph.D. from the same university. His Ph.D. work was in collaboration with CEERI, Pilani, and he has worked in a number of ISRO-sponsored projects. He has designed and conducted a number of training programs for the corporate sector and has served as a trainer for various Government of India departments. Along with six books, he has published more than 100 research papers in various national and international conferences and journals. He was Editor of the international refereed journal *Asia-Pacific Business Review* from June 2007 to June 2009. He is a regular reviewer for a number of international journals and prestigious conferences. He is currently Professor at the Sharda University, Greater Noida, and Visiting Professor at the Indian Institute of Management, Indore, and University of Northern Iowa, USA.

Dr. R. Vidhyalakshmi received her master's in computer science from Bharathidasan University, Tamil Nadu, India, and Ph.D. from JJT University, Rajasthan, India. Her Ph.D. work focused on determining the reliability of SaaS applications. She is a Lifetime Member of ISTE. She has conducted training programs in Java, Advanced Excel, and R Programming. She has published numerous research papers in Scopus indexed international journals and various national and international conference proceedings. Her areas of interest include: information systems, web technologies, database management systems, data sciences, big data and analytics, and cloud computing. She is currently Faculty Member at the Army Institute of Management and Technology, Greater Noida, India.

About the Authors

Chapter 1
Cloud Computing

Abbreviations

CapEx	Capital expenditure
CSA	Cloud security alliance
CSP	Cloud service provider
IaaS	Infrastructure as a service
NIST	National Institute of Standards and Technology
OpEx	Operational expenses
PaaS	Platform as a service
SaaS	Software as a service
SAN	Storage area network

Moore's Law was predicted by Gordon Moore, Intel co-founder in 1965 which stated that the processing power (i.e., number of in a transistor of a silicon chips) will be doubled in every 18–24 months. This became reality only in a few decades and finally failed due to technology advancements resulting in abundant computing power. The processing power doubled in a much less than the expected time and got leveraged in almost all domains for incorporating speed, accuracy, and efficiency. Integrated circuit chips have a limit of 12 mm^2, tweaking the transistors within this limit has also got an upper limit. Correspondingly, the benefits of making the chips smaller is diminishing and operating capacity of the high-end chips has been on the plateau since middle of 2000. This led to a lookout for the development in computing field, beyond the hardware. One such realization is the new computing paradigm called Cloud Computing. Since its introduction about a decade ago, cloud computing has evolved at a rapid pace and has found an inevitable place in every business operation. This chapter provides an insight to various aspects of cloud computing, its business benefits along with real time business implementation examples.

V. Kumar and R. Vidhyalakshmi, *Reliability Aspect of Cloud Computing Environment*, https://doi.org/10.1007/978-981-13-3023-0_1

1.1 Introduction

Most commonly stated definition of cloud computing as provided by NIST is "*Cloud computing is a model for enabling ubiquitous, convenient, on-demand network access to a shared pool of configurable computing resources (e.g. networks, servers, storage, applications and services) that can be rapidly provisioned and released with minimal management effort or service provider interaction*".

Cloud computing has brought disruption in the computing world. All resources required for computing are provided as service over Internet on demand. The delivery of software as a product has been replaced by provision of software as a service. The computing services are commoditized and delivered as utilities. This has brought the idea of John McCarthy into reality. He had suggested in 1961 at MIT's centennial speech that computing technology might lead to a future where the applications and computing power could be sold through utility business model like water or electricity. The maturity of Internet Service Provider (ISP) over a span of time has led to the evolution of cloud computing.

More and more organizations have moved to or willing to move to cloud due to its numerous business benefits, with the main benefit being its innovative approach to solve business problem with less initial investment. Dynamism of technology and business needs have led to tremendous development in cloud computing. Organizations cannot afford to spend days or months in adopting new technology. Keeping abreast with the ever-changing technology will give competitive edge to the organization. If the technology needs of the organization are given keen importance then they may loose out in business innovation, which will eventually push them out of the market. This bottle neck situation is solved by cloud adoption as the technical overhead of the organization is moved on to the Cloud Service Provider (CSP).

Depending on the IT skill strength and finance potential, organizations have various options to fulfill IT needs of the organization like in-house development, hosted setup, outsourcing, or cloud adoption. Most of the organizations prefer hybrid approach for leveraging IT supports from multiple sources depending on the sensitivity of the business operation. This is considered as an optimal strategy for IT inclusion in business as hybrid approach reduces dependency on a single IT support.

1.1.1 Characteristics

Cloud Computing services are delivered over the Internet. It provides a very high level of technology abstraction, due of which, customers with a very limited technical knowledge, can also starts using cloud applications at the click of the mouse. NIST describes characteristics of cloud computing as follows (NIST 2015):

i. *Broad Network Access*
Cloud computing facilitates optimal utilization of computing resources of the organization by hosting them in cloud network and allow access by various departments using wide range of devices. Cloud adoption also facilitates resources and services to be used at the time of need. The services can be utilized using standard mechanism and thin client over Internet from any device. Heterogeneous client platforms are available for access using desktops, laptops, mobiles, and tablet PCs with the help of IE, Chrome, Safari, Firefox, or any browsers that supports HTML standards.

ii. *On-demand Self Service*
Resource requirements for IT implementations in organizations vary according to the specific business needs. Thus, the resources need to be provisioned as per the varying needs of the organization. Faster adoption to changes will provide competitive advantage, which in turn brings agility to the organizations. Usage of traditional computing model to accommodate changing business needs depends on the prediction of business growth. This might end up in either over allocation or under allocation of resources, if the prediction goes wrong. Over allocation leads to under-utilization of resources and under allocation leads to loss of business. Cloud adoption solves these issues as the resources are provisioned based on the current business demands and are released once the demand recedes.

iii. *Elasticity and Scalability*
On-demand resource allocation characteristics bring in two more important characteristics of cloud computing: elasticity and scalability. These characteristics provide flexibility in using the resources. An application, which is initiated to work on a single server, might scale up to 10 or 100 servers depending on the usage which is the elasticity of applications. Scalability is the automatic provisioning and de-provisioning of resources depending on the spikes and surges in IT resource requirements. Scalability can further be categorized as horizontal and vertical scalability. Horizontal scalability refers to the increase in same type of resources, whereas vertical scalability refers to the scaling of resources of various types.

iv. *Measured Services*
Cloud adoption eliminates the traditional way of software or IT resources purchasing, installing, maintenance, and upgrading. IT requirement of the organization are leveraged as services being provided by the CSP. Services are measured and the charges are levied based on subscription or pay-per-use models. Low-investment characteristic of cloud computing helps the startups to leverage IT services with minimal charges. Cloud services can be monitored, measured, controlled, billed, and reported. Effective monitoring is the key to utilize cloud service cost.

v. *Multi-tenancy*
This is the backbone feature of cloud computing allows various users also referred to as tenants, to utilize same resources. A single instance of software application will be used to serve multiple users. These are hosted, provisioned and managed by cloud service providers. The tenants are provided minimum

customization facility. This feature increases optimal utilization of resources and hence reduces usage cost. This characteristic is common in public cloud deployments. The resources allotted to tenants are protected using various isolation techniques.
Software or a solution provided with cloud computing service tag must exhibit all or some of the characteristics defined. Any software product marketed as cloud solution which does not possess these characteristics is referred to as *cloud-washing*.

1.1.2 Deployment Methods

Cloud services can be deployed in any one of the four ways such as private cloud, public cloud, community cloud and hybrid cloud. Physical presence of the resources, security levels, and access methods varies with service deployment type. The selection of cloud deployment method is done based on the data sensitivity of the business and their business requirements (Liu et al. 2011). Figure 1.1 depicts advantages of various deployment methods.

i. Private Cloud
It is cloud setup that is maintained within the premises of the organization. It is also called as "Internal Cloud". Third party can also be involved in this to host an on-site private cloud or outsourced private cloud maintained exclusively for a single organization. This type of deployment is preferred by large organizations that include a strong IT team to setup, maintain, and control cloud operations. This is intended for a single tenant cloud setup with strong data security capabilities. Availability, resiliency, privacy, and security are the major advantages of this type of deployment. Private cloud can be setup using major service providers such as Amazon, Microsoft, VMware, Sun, IBM, etc. Some of the open source implementations for the same are Eucalyptus and OpenSatck.

ii. Public Cloud
This type of cloud setup is open to general public. Multiple tenants exist in this cloud setup which is owned, managed, and operated by service providers. Small- and mid-sized companies opt for this type of cloud deployments with the prime intention to replace CapEx with OpEx. "Pay as you go" model is used in this setup, where the consumers pay only for the resources that are utilized by them. Adoption of this facility eliminates prediction and forecasting overhead of IT infrastructure requirements. Public cloud includes thousands of servers spanning across various data centers situated across the globe. Facility to choose the data center near to their business operations is provided to the consumers to reduce latency in service provisioning. The public cloud setup requires huge investment so it is set up large enterprises like Amazon, Microsoft, Google , Oracle, etc.

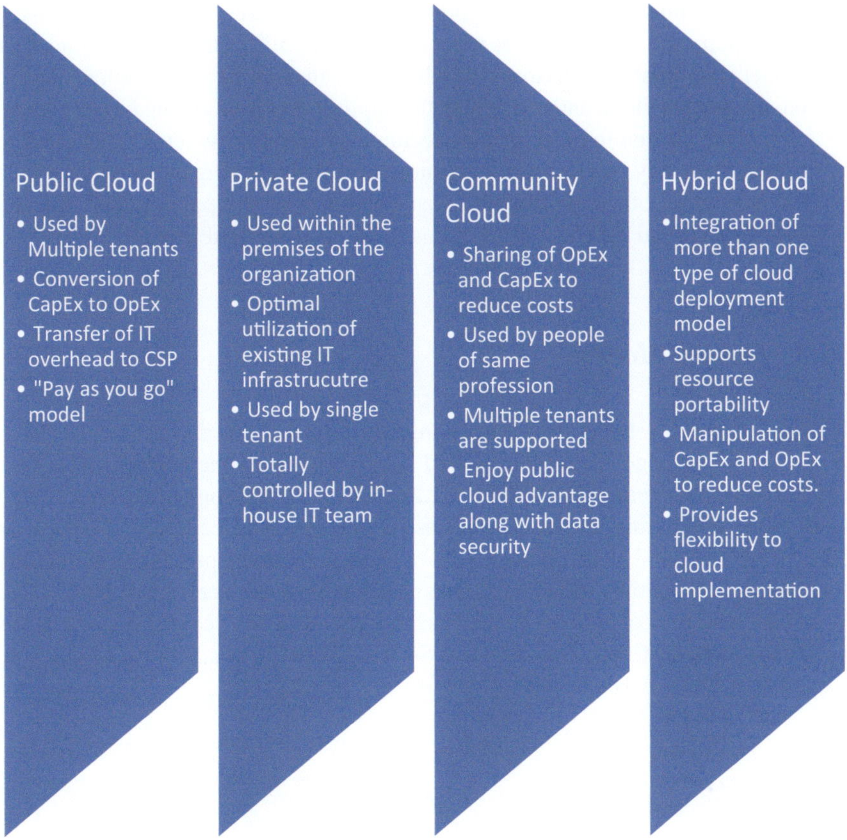

Fig. 1.1 Advantages of various cloud deployments

iii. Community Cloud
This deployment has multi-tenant cloud setup, which is shared by organizations having common professional interest and have common concerns towards privacy, security, and regulatory compliances. This is maintained as an in-house community cloud or outsourced community cloud. Organizations involved in this type of setup will have optimal utilization of their resources as unused resources of one organization will be allotted to the other organization, which is in need of such resources. This also helps to share in-house CapEx of IT resources. Community Cloud setup helps to have advantages of public cloud like Pay-as-you-go billing structure, scalability and multi-tenancy along with the benefits of private cloud such as compliance, privacy, and security.

iv. Hybrid Cloud
This deployment uses integration of more than one cloud deployment model such as on-site or outsourced private cloud, public cloud, and on-site or out-

sourced community cloud. It is preferred in such cases where it is necessary to maintain the facility of one model and also to utilize the feature of another model. The organizations that deal with more sensitive data can maintain data in on-site private cloud and can utilize the applications from public cloud. Hybrid clouds are chosen to meet specific technology or business requirement and to optimize privacy and security at minimum investment. Organizations can take the advantage of scalability, and cost efficiency of the public cloud without exposing critical data and applications to security vulnerabilities.

1.1.3 Service Models

Software, storage, network, and processing capacity are provided as services from cloud. The wide range of services offered is built on top of one another and is also termed as *cloud computing stack*. Figure 1.2 represents cloud computing stack. Three major cloud computing services are Infrastructure as a Service (IaaS), Platform as a Service (PaaS), and Software as a Service (SaaS). With the proliferation of cloud in almost all computing related activities various other services are also provided on demand and are collectively termed as Anything as a Service (XaaS). The XaaS service list includes Communication as a Service, Network as a Service, Monitoring as a Service, Storage as a Service, Database as a Service, etc.

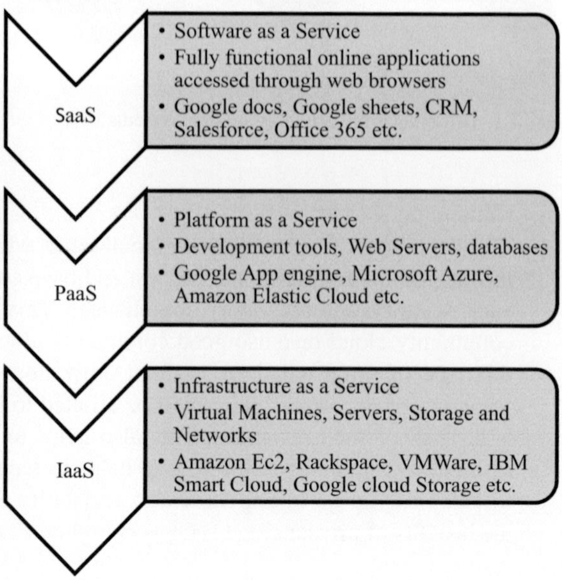

Fig. 1.2 Cloud computing stack showing the cloud service models

i. *Infrastructure as a Service (IaaS)*
This type of computing model provides the virtualized computing resources, such as: servers, network, storage, and Operating System on demand over Internet. Third-party service providers host these resources, which can be utilized by cloud users on subscription basis. The consumers do not have control on the underlying physical resources, but can control operating system, storage and deployed applications. Service providers also perform the associated support tasks like backup, system updation, and resiliency planning. Facility of automatic provisioning and releasing facilitate dynamic resource allocation based on business needs.
A hypervisor or virtual machine monitor (vmm), such as: Xen, Oracle virtual box, VMware, or Hyper-V, creates and runs the virtual machines. These virtual machines are also called as guest machines (Janakiram 2012). A hypervisor provides virtual operating platform to the guest operating system and also manages the execution of guest operating system. A pool of hypervisors with large number of virtual machine provides the scalability. After provisioning of the required infrastructure, the operating system images and application software needs to be installed by the cloud user to use these services. Dynamic scaling of resources, resource distribution as a service, utility pricing model, and handling multiple users on single hardware are the essential characteristics of IaaS. It is preferred organizations with low capital investments, rapid growth, and temporary need of resources or applications that require volatile demand of resources.
IaaS is not preferable when the organizations have compliance regulatory issues in outsourcing or the applications require dedicated devices to provide high performance.
Example: Rackspace, VMware, IBM Smart Cloud, Amazon EC2, Open Stack, etc.

ii. *Platform as a Service (PaaS)*
This type of service provides the software development platform with operating system, database, programming language execution environment, web server, libraries, and tools. These services are utilized to deploy, manage, test, and execute customized applications in cost-effective manner without hardware and software maintenance complexities. Cloud users do not have control on the underlying infrastructure, however has control over the deployed applications. Specialized applications of PaaS are iPaaS, and dPaaS. iPaaS is an Integration Platform as a Service which enables customers to develop and execute integration flows. dPaaS is Data Platform as a Service which provides data management as a service. Data visualization tools are used to retain control and transparency over data.
Providing various easy to deploy UI scenarios using web-based user interface creation tools, enabling utilization of the same development application by multiple users with the help of multi-tenant architecture, providing web services, and database integration using common standards and providing project planning and communication tools for development team collaboration are the main characteristics of PaaS.

PaaS is preferred, when multiple developers are involved in a single project development or in development of applications to leverage the data from the existing application or in the application development using agile software development. It is not preferred in the scenarios, where proprietary language approaches would impact the software development or greater customization of the software and the underlying hardware is unavoidable.
Example: Google app engine, Windows Azure, force.com, Heroku.

iii. *Software as a Service*
Software as a Service abbreviated as SaaS is also called as on-demand software. It is an Internet model based software delivery that has changed the identity of the software from product to service. SaaS applications have resemblance with web services in terms of remote access but the variations are pricing model, software scope, and service delivery of both software and hardware. The providers install and manage application in their cloud infrastructure and cloud user access them using web browsers which are also called as thin clients. The Cloud users have no control on the infrastructure or the application barring few user—specific application configuration settings. This eliminates the cumbersome installation process and also simplifies the maintenance and support. The applications are provisioned at the time of need and are charged based on subscription. As the cloud applications are centrally hosted, software updations are released without the need to perform any reinstallation of the software.
Essential characteristics of SaaS are software delivery as "one-to-many" model, software upgrades and patches handling by cloud provider, Web access provision for commercial software and API interface between pieces of software. SaaS is preferable for applications that have common business operations across the user base, web or mobile access requirements, business operation spikes that prompt resource demand spikes, short-term application software usage requirements. SaaS is not preferable when the applications deal with fast processing of real-time data; legalization issues with respect to data hosting or when the on-premise application satisfies all the business requirements.
Example: Google Docs, Office 365, NetSuite, IBM LotusLive etc.

1.1.4 Virtualization Concepts

Virtualization was introduced in 1960s by IBM for boosting utilization of large expensive mainframes. Now it has regained its usage as one of the core technology of cloud computing which allows abstraction of fundamental elements of computing resources such as server, storage, and networks (Buyya et al. 2013). In simpler terms, it is the facility by which virtual version of the devices or resources such as server, storage, network, or operating system can be created in a single system. It will also help to work beyond the physical IT infrastructure capacity of the organization. The various working environment created are called as virtual because they simulate the interface of the new environment. A computer having Windows operating system can

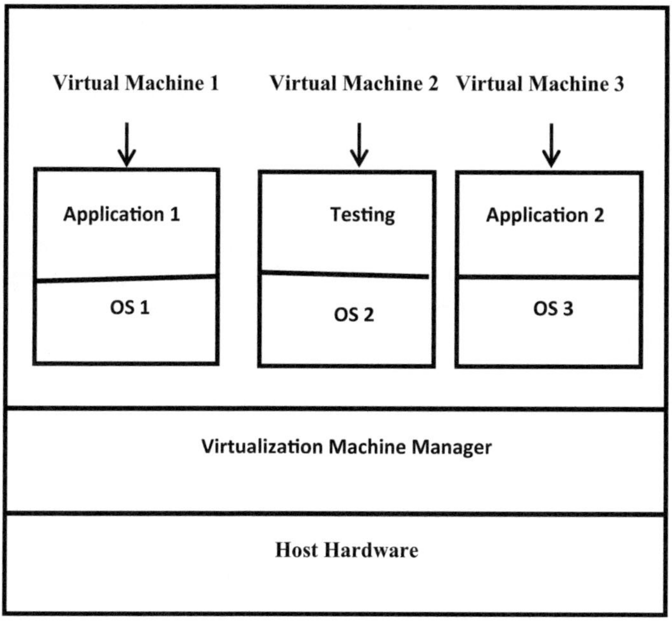

Fig. 1.3 Virtualization on a single machine

be made to work with other operating systems also using virtualization. It increases utilization of hardware resources and also allows organizations to reduce the enormous power consuming servers. This also helps organizations to achieve green IT (Menascé 2005).

VMware and Oracle are the leading companies which are providing products such as VMware Player and Oracle's VirtualBox that supports virtualization implementation. Virtualization can be achieved as a hosted approach or using hypervisor architecture. In hosted approach partitioning services are provided on top of the existing operating system to support wide range of guest operating systems. Hypervisor also known as Virtualization Machine Manager (VMM) is the software that helps in successful implementation of virtualization on the bare machine. It has direct access to the machine hardware and is an interface and a controller between the hosting machine and the guest operating system or applications to regulate the resource usage (vmware 2006).

Virtualization can also be used to combine resources from multiple physical resources into a single virtual resource. Virtualization helps to eliminate server sprawl, reduced complexity in maintaining business continuity, and rapid provisioning for test and development. Figure 1.3 describes the virtualized environment. Various types of virtualizations include

i. Storage virtualization
   It is the combination of multiple network storage devices to project as a single huge storage unit. The storage spaces of several interconnected devices are combined into a simulated single storage space. It is implemented using software on Storage Area Network (SAN), which is a high-speed sub-network of shared storage devices primarily used for backup and archiving processes.
ii. Server virtualization
   The concept of one physical dedicated server is replaced with virtual servers. Physical server is divided into many virtual servers to enhance optimal utilization. Main identity of the physical server is masked and the users interact through the virtual servers only. Usage of virtual web servers helps to provide low-cost web hosting facility. This also conserves infrastructure space as several servers are replaced by a single server. The hardware maintenance overhead is also reduced to a larger extent (Beal 2018).
iii. Operating system virtualization
   This type of virtualization allows the same machine to run the multiple instances of different operating system concurrently through the software. This helps a single machine to run different application requiring different operating system. Another type of virtualization involving OS is called as Operating System-level virtualization where a single OS kernel will provide support for multiple applications running in different partitions of a single machine.
iv. Network virtualization
   This is achieved through logical segmentation of the physical network resources. The available bandwidth is divided into different channels with each being separated and distinguished from each other. These channels will be assigned to server or device for further operations. The true complexity of the network is abstracted and are provided as simple hard drive for usage.

1.1.5 Business Benefits

Cloud adoption gives a wide array of benefits to business like reduced CapEx, greater flexibility, business agility, increased efficiency, enhanced web presence, faster time to market, enhanced collaboration, etc. The business benefits of cloud adoption include

i. Enhanced Business Agility

Cloud adoption enables organizations to handle business dynamism without complexity. This enhances the agility of the organizations as it is equipped to accommodate the changing business and customer needs. The cloud adoption keeps the organization in pace with the new technology updations with minimal or no human interaction. This is achieved through faster and self-provisioning and de-provisioning of IT resources at the time of need from anywhere and using any type of devices. New application inclusion time has reduced from months to minutes.

ii. Pay-As-You-Go

This factor is abbreviated as PYAG is a feature that allows the customers to pay for the resources based on the time and amount of its utilization. Cloud services are meter-based where usage-based payment is done or it is subscription-based. This convenient payment facility enables customers to concentrate on core business activities rather than worrying about the IT investments. The IT infrastructure investment planning is replaced with planning for successful cloud migration and efficient cloud adoption. This useful factor of cloud entitles the new entrants to leverage the entire benefit of ICT implementation with minimal investment.

iii. Elimination of CapEx

This is an important cost factor that eradicates one of the most important barriers to cost-based IT adoption for small businesses. The strenuous way of traditional software usage in business includes activities like purchasing, installing, maintaining, and upgrading. This is simplified to a simple browser usage. User need not worry about the initial costs such as purchase costs, costs related to updation and renewal. In fact the user needs to worry only about the Internet installation cost only in terms of Capex. The software required for the organizations are used directly from the provider's site using authenticated login ids. This eliminates huge initial investment.

iv. Predictable and Manageable Costs

All cloud services are metered and this enables the customer to have greater control on the use of expensive resources. The basic IT requirements of the business have to be observed before cloud adoption and the allocations are to be done only for the basic requirements. This controls the huge initial investment. Careful monitoring of the cloud usage will enable the organizations to predict the financial implications of their cloud usage expansion plans. Huge capital investment on resources that may not be fully utilized is replaced with operation expenses by paying only for the resources utilized thus managing the costs.

v. Increased Efficiency

This refers to the optimal utilization of IT-related resources which will in turn prevent the devices from being over provisioned or under provisioned. Traditional IT resource allocations for server, processing power, and storage are planned by targeting the resource requirement spikes that occur during peak business seasons which last for few parts of a year. These additional resources remain idle for most part of the year thus reducing IT resource efficiency. For example, the estimated server utilization rate is 5–15% of its total capacity. Cloud adoption eliminates the need of over investment on resources. The required resources are provisioned at the time of need and are paid as per usage capacity. This increases the resource efficiency .

vi. Greater Business Continuity

The business continuity is maintained by enhanced disaster recovery management processes that are carried out by cloud providers. Regular backup of data is carried out as it is required to be used by the recovery process at the time of failure. The backup process interval depends on the data intensity of the enterprise. Data intensive applications require daily backup where as others applications require periodic backup. Cloud adoption relieves the users from the traditional cumbersome backup and recovery process. Cloud service adoption includes automatic failover process which guarantees business continuity at faster pace and reduced cost. Mirroring or replication processes are used for backup purpose depending on the intensity of data transactions. The replication of the transactions and storage are easily possible due to server consolidation and virtualization techniques.

vii. Web Collaboration

Interaction between different entities of the organization is established with the help of this factor. The interaction with the customers enables to setup "customer-centric" business. The requirements and feedback gathered from the customers are used as the base for new product or service planning or for the improvement of the existing product or services. Enterprises use this factor to enhance their web presence which will help to gain the advantage of global reach. This also enables the organization to build open and virtual business processes.

viii. Increased Reliability

Any disruption to the IT infrastructure will affect the business continuity and might also result in financial losses. In traditional IT setup, periodic maintenance of the hardware, software, storage, and network are essential to avoid the losses. The reliability of traditional ICT for enterprise operations is associated with risk as the retrieval of the affected IT systems is a time consuming process. Cloud adoption increases the IT usage reliability for enterprise operations by improving the uptime and faster recovery from unplanned outages. This is achieved through live migrations, fault tolerance, storage migrations, distributed resource scheduling, and high availability.

ix. Environment Friendly

Cloud adoption assists the organization to reduce their carbon footprint. Organizations invest on huge servers and IT infrastructure to satisfy their future needs. Utilization of these huge IT resources and heavy cooling systems contribute to the carbon footprint. On cloud adoption the over provisioning of resources are eliminated and only the required resources are utilized from the cloud thus reducing the carbon footprint. The cloud data center working also results in increased carbon footprint but is being shared by multiple users and the providers also employ natural cooling mechanism to reduce the carbon footprint.

x. Cost Reduction

Cloud adoption reduces cost in many ways. The initial investment in proprietary software is eliminated. The overhead charges such as data storage cost, quality control cost, software and hardware updation and maintenance cost are eliminated. The expensive proprietary license costs such as license renewal cost and additional license cost for multiple user access facility is completely removed in cloud adoption.

1.2 Cloud Adoption and Migration

Most of the big organizations have already adopted cloud computing and many of the medium and small organizations are also in the path of adopting cloud. Gartner's has mentioned in 2017 report that Cloud computing is projected to increase to $162B in 2020. As of 2017, nearly 74% of Chief Financial Officers believe Cloud computing will have the most measurable impact on their business. Cloud spending is growing at 4.5 times since 2009 and is expected to grow at a better rate of six times from 2015 through 2020 (www.forbes.com). As with two sides of a coin, cloud adoption also has both merits and demerits. Complexity does exist in choosing between the service models (IaaS, SaaS, PaaS) and deployment models (private, public, hybrid, community). SaaS services can be used as utility services without any worry about the underlying hardware or software, but other services need careful selection to enjoy the complete benefits of cloud adoption. This section deals with various aspects to understand before going for cloud adoption or migration.

1.2.1 Merits of Cloud Adoption

Business benefits of cloud adoption such as cost reduction, elimination of CapEx, leveraging IT benefits with less investment, enhanced web presence, increased business agility, etc., were discussed in Sect. 1.1.5. Some of the general merits and demerits of cloud adoption are

i. Faster Deployments

Cloud applications are deployed faster than on-premise application. This is because the cumbersome process of installation and configuration is replaced by a registration and subscription plan selection process. On-premise applications are designed, created, and implemented for specific customer and had to go through the complete software development life cycle that spans for months. The updation process also had to go through the time consuming development cycle. In contrast to this, the cloud application adoption takes less time as the software is readily available with the provider. The time taken for the initial software usage is reduced from months to minutes. Automatic software integration is another benefit of cloud adoption. This will help people with less technical knowledge to use cloud applications without any additional installation process. Even organizations with existing IT infrastructure and in-house applications can migrate to cloud after performing the required data migration process.

ii. Multi-tenancy

This factor is responsible for the reduced cost of the cloud services. Single instance of an application is used by multiple customers called as tenants. The cost of the software development, maintenance, and IT infrastructure incurred by the CSP is shared by multiple users which results in delivery of the software at low cost. The tenants are provided with the customization facility of the user interface or business rule but not the application code. This factor streamlines the software patches or updates release management. The updations done on the single instance are reflected to all the customers thus eliminating the version compatibility issue with the software usage. This multi-tenancy increases the optimal utilization of the resources thus reducing the resource usage cost for the individuals.

iii. Scalability

In traditional computing methods, organizations plan their IT infrastructure to accommodate the requirement spikes that might happen once or twice a year. Huge cost needs to be spent in purchasing high end systems and storage. Additional maintenance charges needs to be borne by the organization to keep the systems running even during in its idle time. These issues are totally eliminated due to the scalability features in cloud adoption. IT resources that are required for business operations can be provisioned from cloud at the time of need and can be released after the usage. This helps organizations to eliminate the IT forecasting process. Additional IT infrastructure requirements can be scaled horizontally or vertically during seasonal sales or project testing can be handled by dynamic provisioning of resources at the time of need. Including additional number of resources of same capacity to satisfy business needs is called as horizontal scaling. For example, addition of more servers with same capacity to handle web traffic during festive season sales. Increasing the capacity of the provisioned infrastructure is called as vertical scaling. For example, increasing CPU or RAM capacity of the server to handle the additional hits to a web server.

iv. Flexibility

Cloud adoption offers unlimited flexibility to usage of IT resources. Compute resources such as storage, server, network, and runtime can be provisioned and de-provisioned based on business requirement. The charges are also billed based on the usage. Organizations using IaaS and PaaS services need to be vigilant in cloud usage as the releasing of additional resources has to be done on time to control additional cost. Dynamic provisioning feature also provides flexibility of work practices.

v. Backup and Recovery

Recovery is an essential process for business continuity which can be achieved successfully with the help of efficient backup process. Clod adoption provides backup facility by default. Depending on the financial viability of the organization either selected business operations or entire business operations can be backed up. For small and medium organizations, backup storage locations must be planned in such a way that core department or critical data are centrally located and are replicated regionally. This helps to mitigate risk by moving the critical data close to the region and their local customers. Primary and secondary backup sites must be geographically distributed to ensure business continuity. Different types of backups according to NIST are full backup, incremental, and differential. Full back up process deals with back up of all files and folders. Incremental backup captures files that were changed or created since last backup. Differential backup deals with capturing changes or new file creation after last full backup (Onlinetech 2013).

Cloud computing also has some associated challenges that are discussed in detail in Sect. 1.3. Solution for handling these challenges are also discussed which needs to be followed to leverage the benefits of cloud computing adoption.

1.2.2 Cost–Benefit Analysis of Cloud Adoption

Cost–Benefit Analysis (CBA) is a process of evaluating the costs and its corresponding benefits of any investment, here in this context it is cloud adoption. This process helps to make decisions for the operations that have calculable financial risks. CBA should also take into the costs and revenue over a period of time including the changes over monetary values depending on the length and time of the project. Calculating Net Present Value (NPV) will help to measure the present profitability of the project by comparing present ongoing cash flow with the present value of the future cash flow. Three main steps to perform CBA are

i. Identifying costs
ii. Identifying benefits
iii. Comparing both

The main cost benefit of cloud adoption is reduced CapEx. Initial IT hardware and infrastructure expenses are eliminated. This is due to the virtualization and consolidation characteristics of cloud adoption. Various costs associated with cloud adoption are server cost, storage cost, application subscription cost, cost of power, network cost, etc. The pricing model of cloud (Pay-as-you-go) is one of the main drivers for cloud adoption. The costs incurred in cloud adoption can be categorized as upfront cost, ongoing costs and service termination costs (Cloud standards council 2013). Table 1.1 lists the various costs associated with cloud computing adoption.

Various financial metrics such as Total Cost Ownership (TCO), Return on Investment (ROI), Net Present value (NPV), Internal Rate of Return (IRR), and payback

Table 1.1 Various costs associated with cloud adoption

Costs details	Descriptions
Infrastructure setup cost	Cost involved in setting up of hardware, network and purchasing of software
Cloud consultancy charges	This cost will be incurred by organizations not having strong IT team to do IT evaluation
Integration charges	These are the charges for migrating the existing application to cloud or combining in-house applications with the new cloud applications
Customization or reengineering costs	These are the charges that are incurred for the process of changing the existing SaaS applications to suit the business needs or changing of business needs to that of the application requirement
Training costs	An essential cost factor that is required to have complete control on cloud usage and monitoring
Subscription costs	Monthly, quarterly or annual subscription charges for usage of cloud services
Connectivity costs	Network connectivity charges without which cloud service delivery is not possible
Risk mitigation costs	Costs incurred in the alternative measures undertaken to avoid or reduce the adverse effects on business continuity due to outage
Data security costs	Costs of any additional security measures undertaken apart from the basic security offered by the providers
New application identification and installation costs	Costs incurred in selection of new service provider and application on termination of an existing service
Data migration cost	The cost of data transfer from the existing provider to the new provider

period are used to measure the costs and monitor the financial benefits of SaaS investment. ROI is used to estimate the financial benefits of SaaS investment and TCO calculates the total associated direct and indirect costs for the entire life span of SaaS. NPV compares the estimated benefits and costs of SaaS adoption over a specified time period with the help of rate that assist in calculating the present value of the future cash flow. IRR is used to identify the discount rate which would equate the NPV of the investment to zero. ROI calculation being simple when compared to the other metric is preferred for the financial evaluations (ISACA 2012).

Payback period refers to the time taken for the benefits return to equate with that of the investment. Main payback areas of cloud computing where saving and additional costs involved are listed in Table 1.2 (Mayo and Perng 2009).

Table 1.2 Various payback area of cloud computing

Payback area	Cost saving	Additional costs
Software	Reduction in software and OS licenses	Cost of virtualization and cloud management software
Hardware	Reduction in number of servers and facility cost	Nil
Productivity	Reduction in waiting hours for software updates/new services inclusion	Nil
Automated provisioning	Reduction in number of hours of resource provisioning	Training, administration and maintenance of automation software
System administration	Improved productivity due to server consolidation	Nil

1.2.3 Strategy for Cloud Migration

Cloud migration refers to the moving of data and applications related to the business operations from on-premise IT infrastructure to cloud infrastructure. Moving the IT operations from one cloud environment to another is also called as cloud migration. Cisco mentions three types of migration options based on service models—IaaS, PaaS, and SaaS. If an organization switches to SaaS it is not called as migration but is a simple replacement of existing applications. Migrating business applications that were based on standard on-premise application servers to cloud based development environment is done in PaaS migration. This type of PaaS migrations also has various steps such as refactor, revise and rebuild as the existing on-premise applications needs to be modified to suit the cloud architecture and working. IaaS migration deals with migrating applications and data storage on to the servers that are maintained by cloud service provider. This is also called as re-hosting, where existing on-premise applications and data are migrated to cloud (Zhao and Zhou 2014).

Plan, deploy, and optimize are the three main phases that are to be followed for successful cloud migration. Plan phase includes the complete cloud assessment in terms of functional, financial, and technical assessments, identifying whether to opt for IaaS, PaaS, or SaaS and also deciding about the cloud deployment option (public, private, or hybrid). The cost associated with server, storage, network and IT labor has to be detailed and compared with on-premise cloud applications (Chugh 2018). Security and compliance assessment needs to be done to understand the availability and confidentiality of data, prevailing security threats, risk tolerance level, and disaster recovery measures.

Deploy phase deals with application and data migration. The careful planning for porting of the existing on-premise application and its data onto the cloud platform is carried out in this phase so as to reduce or avoid disturbance to business continuity. Either forklift migration where all applications are shifted on to cloud or hybrid migration where partial shifting of application to cloud can be followed.

Self-contained, stateless, and tightly coupled applications are selected and moved in forklift approach. Optimize phase deals with increasing efficiency of data access, auto termination of unused instances, reengineering existing applications to suit cloud environment (CRM Trilogix 2015).

Training the staff to utilize cloud environment is very essential to take control of the fluctuating cloud expenses. The dynamic provisioning helps to cater to the sudden increase in work load and the payment for the same will be done in subscription based model. At the same time continuous monitoring has to be done to scale down the resource requirement when the demand surges. This will help to reap the complete cost benefit of cloud adoption. Unmanaged open source tools or provider based managed tools are available for error free cloud migrations.

Some of the major migration options are live migration, host cloning, data migration, etc. In live migration, running applications are moved from on-premise physical machines on to cloud without suspending the operations. In data migration synchronization between the on-premise physical storage and cloud storage is carried out. After successful migrations users can leverage cloud usage, monitor and optimize cloud usage pattern using various cloud monitoring tools.

1.2.4 Mitigation of Cloud Migration Risks

Business continuity might be affected due to the disturbances to the existing IT operations of the organization. The existing on-premise IT infrastructure, applications, and data have to be completely or partially migrated to cloud. This might include various risks like affect to business continuity, loss of data, application not working, loss of control on data, etc. Some of the cloud migration risk mitigation measures are

i. Identifying the suitable cloud environment
   Cloud environments such as public, private, community, or hybrid has its own merits and demerits. Identifying the one that is suitable to business is very essential to leverage the benefits of cloud adoption. Depending on the sensitivity of the data the cloud deployment model needs to be selected. Big organizations prefer private cloud as they might have the strong IT team to take care of the cloud installation and their sensitive data will not move out of the organization. This may not be the case with small and medium organization who prefer cloud to get rid of the IT overhead. For such organizations it is better to opt for public cloud. As the public cloud platform is being used by many organizations, they strive hard to maintain best IT infrastructure, cloud application with enhanced data security. These features are provided to small organizations at very low cost. Companies which has done reasonable IT investments and still want leverage the benefits of cloud can opt for hybrid cloud environment. The business functions, its implementations, and existing investment on IT infrastructure need to be studied properly and the suitable cloud environment has to be selected.

ii. Choosing the suitable service model
Service model selection plays a greater role in pre-migration strategy. This selection is completely based on the size of the organization and the existing IT expertise. The organizations which had already invested in IT infrastructure and had been maintaining on-premise applications efficiently but still intend to opt for cloud to accommodate varying storage or server loads can opt for IaaS. The organizations that have ample IT infrastructure to cater to the changing loads but are having issues with software purchases can opt for PaaS where the required development or testing platform is provided as service. New startups or small and medium organizations which are not having huge IT investment can opt for SaaS. This adoption will enable organizations to benefit from IT implementation for their operations without any worry about purchase, installation, maintenance, and renewals. Depending on the utilization the subscription can be taken as monthly, quarterly, or yearly. Most of the SaaS products have trial period within which suitability of the product for business operations can be studied. The monitoring cloud service of any type is essential for subscribing at the time of need and unsubscribing after usage. This will help to keep cloud costs under control.

iii. Identifying the best suitable applications
The business processes needs to be segregated as critical business processes that have to be executed without even a single minute delay and non-critical business processes which are tolerant to delay due to service outages. Non-critical applications are the first choice for cloud adoption. For example real time applications like online games, stock market trading, online bidding, etc., are time bound and needs to be completed on that particular moment without any delay. If these applications are moved to cloud, then any network outage or latency in data provisioning will result in loss of business. Such applications are better if maintained in-house. Organization having good IT team might be in need to implement few operations occasionally. Instead of developing software for those operations, the team can opt for cloud applications which can be subscribed at the time of need and unsubscribed after use. This will eliminate development time and maintenance cost of the software. Small and medium organizations, which are not having IT team, can opt for multiple SaaS application for their operations. Subscribing applications from multiple vendors will eliminate the risk of suffering from outages.

iv. Business continuity plan during migration
This is an essential operation for the organization that have existing IT setup and software for their operations. New entrants in business can omit this step. Ensuring resiliency is a major characteristic of any IT implementation. Hence, it is always advisable to opt for phased manner migrations. This will help organizations to continue their current business operations with tolerable disturbances. Listing of critical and non-critical business operations and its corresponding IT applications have to be done. This will help to identify less critical applications, which are the best candidates to be moved to cloud first. Backup plans must be in place to ensure information availability in case of failed or delayed cloud

migration process. Before migrating to cloud, the data transfer time needs to be calculated. Formula to calculate the number of days that will be taken for data transfer depending on the amount of data to transfer and the network speed is given below (Chugh 2018).

$$\text{No. of days} = \frac{\text{Total bytes}}{(\text{mbps} * 125 * 1000 * \text{network utilization} * 60\,\text{s} * 60\,\text{mins} * 24\,\text{h}}$$

1.2.5 Case Study for Adoption and Migration to Cloud

Industry: Entertainment
Company: Netflix
Source: https://increment.com/cloud/case-studies-in-cloud-migration/

In October 2008, Neil hunt, chief production officer at Netflix had called for a meeting of his engineering staffers. The reason for the meeting was to discuss about the problem that Netflix were facing. Its backend client architecture had some issues. It was a having issues with connections and threads. Even an upgrade to machine worth $5 million crashed immediately as it could not withstand the extra capacity of thread pool. It was a disagreeable position for Netflix as it had introduced online streaming of its video library a year before. It had also partnered with Microsoft to get its app on the Xbox 360, had agreed with TV set-top boxes to service their customers and had agreed to the terms of the manufacturers of Blu-ray players. But their back end could not cope with the load. Public had huge expectation as Netflix concept was viewed as a game changing technology for the industry of online video streaming.

There were two points of failure in the physical technology. A single Oracle data base which on an array of Blade servers where Netflix's database was stored and executed using a single unit of machine. With this setup it is impossible to run the show and hence they have to make it redundant. That is a second data center had to be set to improve the situations. This will remove the single point failure. But they could not go ahead due to the financial crisis of the company. The company tried to push a piece of firmware to the disk array and that had corrupted the Netflix database. The company had to spend three days to recover the data. The meeting called by Hunt had decided to rethink and had decided to do everything from the beginning using Cloud technology.

They had detailed all the issues that was plaguing the smooth functioning of online streaming and were determined that these issues should not re-occur with cloud adoption. No maintenance or physical upkeep of the data centers, flexible way to ensure reliable IT resources, lowering costs, scaling of capacity, and increasing adaptability are the main features required for startups with high unpredictable growth. Netflix being a startup had made a wise decision to migrate to cloud.

Between December 2007 and December 2015, with cloud adoption, the company had achieved one thousand times increase in the number of hours of content streaming. The user sign up has increased eight times. Cloud infrastructure was able to stretch to meet the ever expanding demand. Cloud adoption also proved to be cost-effective.

Since the cloud was young technology in 2006 with Amazon being the leader caution was required. Netflix had decided to move in small steps. It moved a single page onto Amazon Web Services (AWS) to make sure that it works. AWS was chosen over others alternatives due to its breadth of features, scaling capacity and broader variants of APIs. Netflix cloud adoption was at a point when organizations were not fully aware of cloud migration process. The cloud adoption involved lot of out of box thinking. Lack of standards for cloud adoption was a point of concern for Netflix.

Rushlan Meshenberg of Netflix says "running physical data centers are simple as we have to keep our servers up and running at all times and with all cost. That's not the case with the cloud. Software runs on ephemeral instances that aren't guaranteed to be up for any particular duration or at any particular time. You can either lament that ephemerality and try to counteract it, or you can try to embrace it and say—I'm going to build a reliable system on top of something that is not."

Netflix had decided to build a system that can fail in parts but not as a whole. Netflix had built a tool that named Chaos Monkey that would self-sabotage its systems. This will simulate the condition of crash to make sure that their engineers are architect, write and test software that's resilient in times of failures. Meshenberg admits that "In the initial days Chaos Monkey tantrums in the cloud were dispiriting. It was painful, as we didn't have the best practices and so many of our systems failed in production. But this had helped our engineers to build software using best practices that can withstand such destructive testing."

Meshenberg says "The crux of our decision to go into the cloud was simple one. Maintaining and building data centers wasn't our core business. It is not something from which our users get value from. Our users get value from enjoying their entertainment. We decided to focus on that and push the underlying infrastructure to cloud providers like AWS."

Scalability was the main factor which inspired Netflix to move to cloud. Meshenberg recalls "Every time you grow your business your traffic grows by an order of magnitude. The things that worked on a small scale may no longer work at bigger scale. We made a bet that cloud would be sufficient in terms of capacity and capability to support our business and the rest was figuring out the technical details of how to migrate and monitor."

1.3 Challenges of Cloud Adoption

Internet-based working pattern of cloud inherits the security and continuity risks and these factors also acts as inhibitors for cloud adoption. A careful security and risk management are essential to overcome this barrier. The cloud adoption should not be carried out depending on the market hype but by detailed parsing of the merits and demerits of cloud adoption (Vidhyalakshmi and Kumar 2013).

The challenges of Cloud Computing are categorized based on different perspective as

i. Technology perspective
ii. Provider perspective
iii. Consumer perspective
iv. Governance perspective

1.3.1 Technology Perspective

This category includes challenges raised due to the base technology aspects such as virtualization; Internet-based operations and remote access. High latency, security, insufficient bandwidth, interaction with on-premise applications, bulk data transfer, and mobile access are some of the challenges of this category.

i. High Latency

The time delay between the placing of request to the cloud provider and availability of the service from them is called as latency. Network congestion, packet loss, data encryption, distributed computing, virtualizations of cloud applications, data center location and the load at the data center are the various factors that are responsible for latency. The highly coupled modules which have intense data interactions between them, when being used in distributed computing will result in data storm and hence latency depending on the location of the interacting modules. Latency is a serious business concern as half a second delay will cause 20% drop in Google's traffic and a tenth of a second delay will cause a drop of 1% in Amazon's sales.

Segregating the applications as tolerant to latency and intolerant to latency and maintaining the intolerant applications as on-premise application or opting for hybrid cloud is a suggested solution (David and Jelly 2013). Choosing the data center location near to the enterprise location can also bring down latency.

ii. Security

Distributed computing, shared resources, multi-tenancy, remote access, and third-party hosting are the various reasons that infuse the security challenge in cloud computing (Doelitzscher et al. 2012). Data may be modified or deleted either accidentally or deliberately at the provider's end who have access to the data. Any breach of conduct or privilege misuse by the data center employee will go unnoticed as it is beyond the scope of customer monitoring. Security breaches that were identified in the highly secured fiber optics cable network, data tapping without accessing network are adding more challenges (Jessica 2011). The security concern is with both the data at rest and the data in motion.

Encryption at the customer's end is one of the solutions to the security issues. Distributed identity management has to be maintained using Lightweight Directory Access Protocol (LDAP) to connect to identity systems.

iii. Insufficient Bandwidth

Robust telecommunication infrastructure and network is essential to cater to "anytime, anywhere" access feature of Cloud Computing. Efficient and effective cloud services can be delivered with the help of high-quality- and high-speed network bandwidth. As more and more companies are migrating to cloud services, issues are raised in many company's bandwidth and in server performances.

The technical developments like 4G wireless network, satellites and broadband Next Generation Networks (NGN) have been tested to provide solution for band width issue. Policies must be set to streamline and restrict the cloud service usage for official activities. Network re-architecture and efficient distribution of database will ensure fast data movement between the customer and the data center.

iv. Mobile Access

Pervasive computing which enables the application to be accessed from any type of device also introduce a host of issues such as authentication, authorization, and provisioning. The failure of hypervisor to control the remote devices, mobile connectivity disruptions due to signal failure, stickiness issue because of the frequent application usage switches between PC and mobile devices are the challenges faced due to mobile access.

Topology-agnostic identification of mobile device is essential to gain control and monitor the mobile accesses of the cloud applications. 4G/LTE services with the advantages such as plug and play features, high capacity data storage and low latency will also provide a solution.

1.3.2 Service Provider Perspective

The providers are classified as Cloud Service Providers (CSP) providing IaaS, PaaS, or SaaS services on contractual basis, Cloud Infrastructure Provider (CIP) providing infrastructure support to CSPs and Communication Service Providers providing transmission service to CSPs. Various challenges faced by them are regulatory compliance, Service level agreement, Interoperability, performance monitoring and reporting and environmental concerns.

i. Regulatory Compliance

Providers are expected to be compliant with PCI DSS, HIPAA, SAS 70, SSAE 16, and other regulatory standards to provide a proof of security. This is a challenging task due to the cross border, geographically distributed computing nature of Cloud processes. The other challenge is the huge customer base spanning different industry verticals having varied security requirement levels.

Some of the providers offer the compliance requirements at an increased cost. The pricing of the product varies with the intensity of the compliance requirement.

ii. Service Level Agreement

This is agreement bond between the provider and the customer providing the assurance for service availability, service quality, disaster management facility, and creditability on service failure. It is challenging to design the SLA keeping a balance between provider's business profitability and the customer's service benefits.

The customers should read and understand the SLA thoroughly and must look for the inclusion of security standards specifications, penalty for service disruption, software upgrade intervals, data migration and termination charges.

iii. Interoperability

Providers are expected to design or host applications with horizontal interoperability, a facility for the application to be used with other cloud or on-premise applications and vertical interoperability, a facility that allows the application to be used with any type of devices. The switching of cloud applications from one provider to another is also a type of interoperability.

"Device-agnostic" characteristics when implemented on cloud applications will provide a solution for vertical interoperability. Microsoft "Health Vault" is an exemplary example of vertical interoperability implementation. One of the solutions for horizontal interoperability is to streamline the working of organizations across the Globe.

iv. Environmental Concerns

Huge cooling systems used by the data centers maintained by the CSPs and CIPs are the reasons for the environmental concerns. Cloud computing is touted as the best solution to reduce carbon footprint when compared to individual server usage due to its consolidation facility. Still it is responsible for 2% of the world's energy usage.

Close-to-consumer cloud, data center with natural cooling facilities, floating platform-mounted data centers, sea-based electrical generators are various suggestions to reduce the environment impact.

1.3.3 Consumer Perspective

The consumers adopt cloud with the main intention to pass over the IT concerns to the 3rd party and to concentrate on core business operations and innovations. The challenges from their perspective are availability, data ownership, organizational barriers, scalability, data location, and migration.

i. Availability

This is one of the primary concerns for the consumers as any issue with this would affect the business operations and may result in financial and customer reputation losses. It is challenging to enjoy the availability claims by the provider due to the internet based working of the cloud.

The providers take utmost care to make the services available as per their agreement by using replication, mirroring, and live migrations. Critical business operations that need to maintain continuity must opt for replication across the globe. Availability is an important focus of the cloud performance and hence an integral part of all the Service Level Agreements.

ii. Organizational Barriers

The complexity of the business is a very big challenge for cloud adoption. Organizations that deal with sensitive data, highly critical time-based processing, complex interdependency between working modules face a major challenge to migrate to cloud. Organization's non-willingness to mend its working to suit with the cloud operations is a major challenge for cloud adoption.

Cloud Service Brokers (CSB) plays a major role is such situations to provide a hybrid solution to maintain the organization working and also to leverage the cloud benefits.

iii. Scalability

This is one of the primary benefits of cloud, which helps the startups to utilize the ICT facilities depending on their business requirements and is also a great challenge to monitor regularly. Auto-deployment option accommodates the user requirement spikes with extra resources at an additional cost. Monitoring the spikes and de-provisioning of the additional resources on spike period completion to reduce the additional cost is a major challenge for the consumers.

IT personnel of the organization must be trained efficiently to handle the dashboard and to constantly monitor the service provided.

iv. Data Location and Migration

The data location might keep changing due to the data center load balancing process or due to data center failures. The consumer can change the provider either because of the service termination of the provider or because of the service discontentment. In any case data have to be migrated where data leaks is a big challenge.

Localization is one of the suggested solutions but this may pioneer issues such as latency due to overload and increased cost due to under-utilization of resources. The option of selecting the data center location can be provided to the customers so that instead of localizing the data the customers can choose the desired locations where the data can be shifted.

1.3.4 Governance Perspective

Geographically distributed working and cross-border provisioning invites challenges as the laws and policies vary across different countries. The challenges are security, sovereignty, and jurisdiction.

i. Sovereignty and Jurisdiction

The challenge is due to the jurisdiction of the location where the data are stored. The countries such as the US and EU have different approaches to privacy. Some countries do not have any strong policy maintained for data protection. EU accepts data export only to such countries which assure adequate level of data protection. The US implies data protection for health and finance data. The protection regimes are mixed outside the US and EU countries. These differences in the data protection laws stage a big challenge for the providers.

The US–EU Safe Harbor is the solution to the data storage and protection. Standards Organizations are regularly amending the data protection laws and policies that are to be incorporated by the providers.

ii. Security

This challenge deals with the security of data from the government access. US Patriot law has a provision to demand data access of any computer. The data would be handed over to the government without the knowledge of the organization.

A large number of the US cloud providers have initiated the need to provide a simpler and clearer standard for the access of personal data and that of electronic communications. Cloud providers have to comply with the standards provided by ISO/IEC to maintain information security.

1.4 Limitations of Cloud Adoption

The working of Cloud Computing like remote access, virtualization, distributed computing, geographically distributed data bases instill limitations in the design and usage of cloud applications. Internet penetration intensity also imposes some limitation on cloud usage as Internet is the base to deliver any type of cloud services. For example the Internet penetration of India is 34.1% (www.internetsociety.org). This eventually limits the cloud usage by Indian users. The other limitations are

i. Customization

Cloud applications are created based on the general requirement of the huge customer base. Customer specific customizations are not possible and this forces the customers to tolerate unwanted modules or to modify their working according to the application requirements. This is one of the main barriers for SMBs to adopt cloud.

ii. Provider Dependency

Total control of the application lies with the provider. Updations are carried out at their pace depending on the global requirements. Incompatible data formats maintained by the providers may force the customer to stick with them. Any unplanned outages will result in financial and customer loss as the business continuity is dependent on the provider.

iii. Application Suitability

The complexity of the application also can limit the cloud usage. The applications with more module interactions that involve intensive data movements between the modules are not suitable for cloud migration. 3D modeling applications when migrated to cloud may experience slow I/O operations due to virtual device drivers (Jamsa 2011). Applications that can be parallelized are more suitable for cloud adoptions.

iv. Non-Scalability of RDBMS

The ACID property based traditional databases do not support share-nothing architecture essential for scalability. Usage of RDBMS for the geographically distributed cloud applications require complex distributed locking and commit mechanism. The traditional RDBMS that has compromise on partition tolerance has to be replaced with shared databases that preserve partition tolerance but compromises on either consistency or availability.

v. Migration from RDBMS to NoSQL

Majority of cloud applications have data processing in peta byte scale and uses distributed storage mechanism. Traditional RDBMS has to be replaced with No SQL to keep pace with the volume of data growing beyond the capacity of the server, variety of data gathered, and the velocity by which it is gathered. The categories of the No SQL databases are Column-oriented databases (Hbase, Google's Big Table and Cassandra), Key-value store (Hadoop, Amazon's Simple DB) and Document-based store (Apache Couch DB, Mongo DB).

1.5 Summary

This chapter outlines the basic characteristics, deployment methods such as public, private, community, hybrid, various service models such as IaaS, PaaS, SaaS. The technical base for cloud adoption (i.e.) concepts of virtualization has also been discussed. This would have given the readers a clear understanding of important aspects with respect cloud computing. Cost is one of the main factors projected as an advantage for cloud adoption. Understanding various costs heads included in cloud adoption are detailed in this chapter. Chapter provides a good understanding to the readers about the essentials to be monitored for cloud cost control. Business benefits of cloud adoption, challenges, and limitations of cloud adoption have also been highlighted. Careful selection of cloud service model and deployment model is essential for leveraging cloud benefits. The metrics that are to be used for cloud service selection and the model to be used to identify reliable cloud service provider are detailed in the succeeding chapters.

References

Beal, V. (2018). Virtualization. https://www.webopedia.com/…/virtualization.html. Accessed on February, 2018.

Buyya, R., Vecchiola, C., & Selvi, S. T. (2013). *Mastering cloud computing* (2nd ed.). McGraw Hill Education (India) Private Limited.

Chugh, S. (2018). On-Premise to Cloud: AWS Migration in 5 Super Easy Steps retrieved from serverguy.com/cloud/aws-migration/ on March 2018.

Cloud Standards Customer Council. (2013). Public Cloud Service Agreements: What to Expect and What to Negotiate. A CSCC March, 2013 article retrieved on November 10, 2014 from http://www.cloud-council.org/publiccloudSLA.pdf.

Columbus, L. (2018). Roundup of Cloud Computing Forecasts, 2017. Retrieved from www.forbes.com accessed on March 29, 2018.

CRM Trilogix. (2015). Migration to cloud, retrieved from pdfs.semanticscholar.org/presentation/5a99 on April 2018.

David, S., & Jelly, F. (2013). Truth and Lies about Latency in the Cloud. White paper from Interxion, retrieved on December 3, 2013 from www.interxion.com.

Doelitzscher, F., Reich, C., Knahl, M., Passfall, A. & Clarke, N. (2012). An agent based business aware incident detection system for cloud environments. *Journal of Cloud Computing, 1*(1), 1–19.

ISACA. (2012). Calculating Cloud ROI: From the Customer Perspective. Retrieved on May 29, 2018 from www.isaca.org/Cloud-ROI.

Jamsa, K. (2011). *Cloud computing: SaaS, PaaS, IaaS, virtualization, business models, mobile, security and more* (pp. 123–125). Jones & Bartlett Publishers.

Janakiram, M. S. V. (2012). Demystifying the Cloud. An e-book retrieved on December 10, 2012 from www.GetCloudReady.com.

Jessica, T. (2011). Connecting Data Centers over Public Networks. IPEXPO.ONLINE article, retrieved on June 12, 2012 from http://online.ipexpo.co.uk/2011/04/20/connecting-data-centres-over-public-networks/.

Liu, F., Tong, J., Mao, J., Bohn, R., Messina, J., Badger, L., et al. (2011). NIST cloud computing reference architecture. *NIST Special Publication, 500*(2011), 292.

Mayo, R., & Perng, C. (2009). Cloud Computing Payback; An explanation of where the ROI comes from, IBM whitepaper November 2009 retrieved on April 23, 2013 from www.ibm.com.

Menascé, D. A. (2005, December). Virtualization: Concepts, applications, and performance modeling. In *International CMG Conference* (pp. 407–414).

NIST Special Publication Article. (2015). Cloud Computing Service Metrics Description. An article published by NIST Cloud Computing Reference Architecture and Taxonomy Working Group, retrieved on September 12, 2015 from http://dx.doi.org/10.6028/NIST.SP.307.

Onlinetech whitepaper. (2013). Disaster Recovery. Retrieved from http://web.onlinetech.com on February, 2018.

Vidhyalakshmi, P., & Kumar, V. (2013). Cloud computing challenges & limitations for business applications. *Global Journal of Business Information Systems, 1*(1), 7–20.

Vmware. (2006). Virtualization Overview. Vmware whitepaper accessed from www.vmware.com on April, 2018.

Zhao, J. F., & Zhou, J. T. (2014). Strategies and methods for cloud migration. *International Journal of Automation and Computing, 11*(2), 143–152.

Chapter 2
Cloud Reliability

Abbreviation

BC	Business continuity
IA	Information availability
MTTF	Mean time to failure
MTTR	Mean time to recovery
MTBF	Mean time between failure
ERP	Enterprise resource planning
SRE	Software reliability engineering

Reliability is a tag that can be attached to any product or service delivery. Mere attachment of this tag will exhibit the perceived characteristics such as trustworthiness and consistent performance. This tag becomes more important for the cloud computing environments, due to its strong dependence on internet for its service delivery. Cloud adoption eliminates IT overhead, but it also brings in security, privacy, availability, and reliability issues. Based on the survey by Juniper Research Agency, the number of worldwide cloud service consumers is projected to be 3.6 billion in 2018. Cloud computing market is flooded with numerous cloud service providers. It is a herculean task for the consumers to choose a CSP to best suit their business needs. Possessing reliability tag for services will help CSPs to outshine their competitors. This chapter deals with the reliability aspect of cloud environments. Various reliability requirements with respect to business along with basic understanding of cloud reliability concepts are detailed in this chapter.

2.1 Introduction

Reliability is defined as the probability of the product or service to work up to the satisfaction of the customer for a given period of time. It is a metric that is used

V. Kumar and R. Vidhyalakshmi, *Reliability Aspect of Cloud Computing Environment*, https://doi.org/10.1007/978-981-13-3023-0_2

to measure the quality of a product or service and it also highlights trustworthiness or dependability of the same. The main aim of reliability theory is to predict when the system will fail in the near future. It is highly user-oriented and also depends on how the product or service is being used by a particular user. Let us consider an example of mobile phone with the features such as 12MP rear and 5MP front camera, 5.5 in. display, latest Qualcomm processor and latest android Operating System. Manufacturing and testing of a mobile will be done as per the standard specifications and will be launched in the market. All prospective customers of the mobile will not grade this mobile as same. Some may consider it as a best mobile, handy to use mobile with good battery life. Some may feel the processor is little slow, screen resolution is not satisfactory or the charging is very slow. This variation in grading the phone with same features occurs due to the requirement variations of the individual. Hence, *reliability is user-oriented*. Depending on the user requirements, the weightage for the factors has to be decided by consumers.

This holds true for software product also. Software might be termed as reliable by one set of users and not the same by another set of users. Assume, there are two organizations such as A1 and A2 with same business requirements. The only difference is that the customer base and turnover of A1 is less when compared to A2. A1 had deployed tax calculating application in their organization and had suggested the same to A2 as they were totally satisfied with its working. A2 also deployed the same and found issues with the working of the software. Software that worked perfectly for A1 has fluked for A2 provided both organizations have same business requirement. The only difference is that A1 has usage requirement of 1 h/day and usage requirement of A2 is for the whole day. This is due to the difference in size of their customer base. The software had some memory issues in prolonged continuous usage because of which organization A2 was not finding it reliable. But, the same software was considered as reliable software with respect to organization A1. Hence reliability is usage oriented which in turn is dependent on business requirements. Hence, *reliability is usage centric*. Due to this user-centric approach it becomes difficult to quantify the reliability in absolute terms. Reliability relates with the operations of product or services rather than with the design aspects. Due to this, reliability is often dynamic and not static (Musa et al. 1990).

IEEE reliability society states that reliability is a design engineering discipline that applies scientific knowledge to assure that the system will perform its designated function for a specified duration within a given environment (rs.ieee.org). If the reliability of a system XYZ that runs for 100 h is said to be 0.99, then it means that the probability of the system to work without any failure s 0.99 or the system runs perfectly for 99 out of 100 h. This can also be mentioned as that the system XYZ has the probability of failure as 0.01 or that the system has encountered 0.01 failures in 100 h. The reliability calculation is based on creating a probability density function f of time t. Any failure that leaves the system inoperable or non- mission specific is referred to as *mission reliability*. Failures caused due to minor errors which degrade system performance that can be rectified are called as *basic reliability*. Fault, failure and time are the key concepts of reliability. Fault occurs when the observed outcome of the system is different from the desired outcome. It is the defect in the program

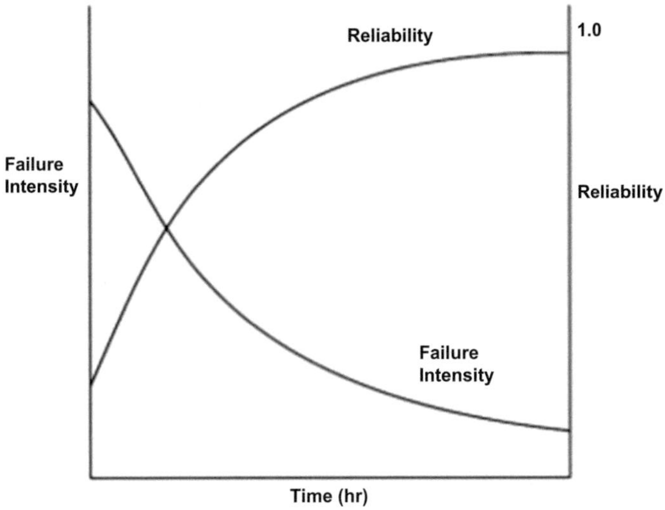

Fig. 2.1 Reliability and failure intensity graph

which when executed under certain conditions will result in failure. In other words, the reason for failure is referred to as fault. Reliability values are always represented as mean value. Various general reliability measuring techniques are (Aggarwal and Singh 2007)

i. Rate of Occurrence of Failure
ii. Mean Time to Failure (MTTF)
iii. Mean Time to Repair (MTTR)
iv. Mean Time Between Failure (MTBF)
v. Probability of Failure on Demand
vi. Availability

The reliability quantities are measured with respect to unit of time. Probability theory is included in the estimation of reliability due to the random nature of failure occurrence. The value of these quantities cannot be predicted as the occurrence of failures is not known with certainty. It differs with the usage pattern. It is represented as cumulative number of failures by time t and *failure intensity,* which is measured as number of failures per unit time t. Figure 2.1 represents reliability and failure intensity graph with respect to time. It is evident from the graph that as the faults are removed from the system after multiple tests and corrections, it gets stabilized. The failure intensity will decrease and hence reliability of the system will increase.

2.1.1 Mean Time Between Failure

Mean time Between Failure (MTBF) is the term that is used to provide amount of failure for a product with respect to time. It is one of the deciding factors as it indicates the efficiency of the product. This factor is essential for the developers or the manufacturer rather than for the consumers. These data are not readily available for the consumers or the end users. This factor is given importance by the consumers only on those products or services that are used for real time or critical operations where failure leads to huge loss.

2.1.2 Mean Time to Repair

Mean Time to Repair abbreviated as MTTR refers to the time taken for repairing a failed system or components. Repairing could be either replacing a failed component or modifying the existing component to adapt with changes or to remove failures that were raised due to faults. Taking long time to repair the product or software shoots up operational cost. Organizations strive to reduce MTTR by having backup plans. This factor is of concern for the consumers as they enquire about the turn-around time for repairing a product.

2.1.3 Mean Time to Failure

Mean Time to Failure (MTTF) denotes the average time for which the device will perform as per specification. The bigger the value the better is the product reliability. It is similar to MTBF but the difference is that MTBF is used with products that can be repaired and MTTF is used for the non-repairable products. MTTF data is collected for a product by running many thousands of units. This metric is crucial for hardware components and that too while they are used in mission critical applications.

2.2 Software Reliability Requirements in Business

Software usage is omnipresent in day-to-day life. It is still more essential in day-to-day business activities. The complexity and usage paradigm of software systems have grown drastically in the past few decades. More and more business establishments irrespective of their size have opted for some type of Enterprise Resource Planning (ERP) implementation. Inclusion of software in business operations has helped organizations to enhance productivity, efficiency and to gain competitive advantage. With the growing Internet penetration and development of cloud computing, organizations have opportunity to promote their web presence which will help them to capture global market (i.e.) help them to do business across boundaries. This tremendous advantage of software implementation also has a flip side. Due to the dependency on software for business operations, software failures can lead to major business break down which will result in financial and reputation loss for the organization (Lyu 2007).

IEEE 982.1-1988 defines software reliability as "The ability of the system or component to perform its required functions under stated conditions for a specified period of time". The dependability of software relies on its availability, reliability, safety and security. *Availability* refers to the ability of the system to deliver its services when needed. *Reliability* refers to the ability of system to deliver services as specified in the documentation. *Safety* of the system refers to the execution of the system without any failure. *Security* of the system refers to the ability of the system to protect itself from intentional or unintentional attacks or intrusions (Briand 2010). The levels of software reliability requirement vary with the software usage. For example, software used for real time activities like stock market, online gaming needs higher level of reliability. Comparatively lower level of reliability is required for some office software system.

It is the responsibility of the software developer to provide reliable software. The company should provide software that will meet the requirements of the user for the specified amount of time. The main crux is that the reliable software should be available at the time of need and has to provide right information to the right type of people (Wiley 2010). It is not only the responsibility of the software provider but the organizations should also have business continuity measures to safeguard their financial loss and business reputation. These measures are discussed in Sect. 2.2.1.

2.2.1 Business Continuity

Business Continuity (BC) is an enterprise wide process that encompasses all IT planning activities such as prepare, respond and recover from planned and unplanned outages. Planning involves proactive measure such as analysis of business impact and assessment of risk and reactive measures such as disaster recovery. Backup and replication is used for proactive processes and recovery is used in the reactive process. Information unavailability that results in business disruption could lead to catastrophic effects depending on the criticality of the business. Information may be inaccessible due to natural disaster, planned or unplanned outages. Planned outages may occur due to hardware maintenance, new hardware installation, software upgrades, or patches, backup operations, migration of the applications from testing to the production environment, etc. Unplanned outages occur due to physical or virtual device failures, database failures, unintentional or intentional human errors, etc.

Various activities, entities, and terminologies used in BC are

i. Disaster recovery
It is the process of restoring data, infrastructure and system to support the ongoing business operations. The last copy of data is restored and upgraded to the point of consistency by applying logs and other processes. The recovery completion is followed by validation to ensure data accuracy.
ii. Disaster restart
The data pertaining to the critical business operations are mirrored rather than copied. Mirroring process replicates the data simultaneously to maintain consistency between the original data and its copy. The disaster restart is a process that restarts the business operation with the mirrored copy of data.
iii. Data vault
It is a remote site repository that is used to store periodic or continuous copies of data in tape drives or disks.
iv. Cluster
It is a group of servers and other resources grouped to operate as a single system so as to ensure availability and to perform load balancing. In failover clusters, one server processes the applications and the other is kept as redundant server which will take over on the failure of the main server.
v. Hot site
It is a site with complete set of essential IT infrastructure available at running condition where the enterprise operations can be shifted during disasters.
vi. Cold site
It is a site with minimal IT infrastructure to which an enterprise operation can be shifted during emergencies.
vii. Recovery time objective (RTO)
It specifies the amount of downtime that could be tolerated by the business operations. It is the time within which the system must be restored back to its original working condition. The disaster recovery optimization plans are based on this. Depending on RTO specification the device and the site of recovery are chosen.
viii. Recovery point objective (RPO)
This specifies the point to which the systems must be restored back after an outage. It also specifies the data loss tolerance level of the business. It is used as a base to decide the replication device and procedures.

BC planning has systematic life cycle approach from its conceptualization to actual implementation. The five stages involved in the BC life cycle as illustrated in Fig. 2.2 are (Wiley 2010):

i. Establish objectives
The BC requirements are determined after detailed study of the business operations. The budget for the BC implementations is estimated and viability is assessed. A BC team is formed with internal and external subject area experts from all business fields. The final outcome of this stage is the BC policies draft.

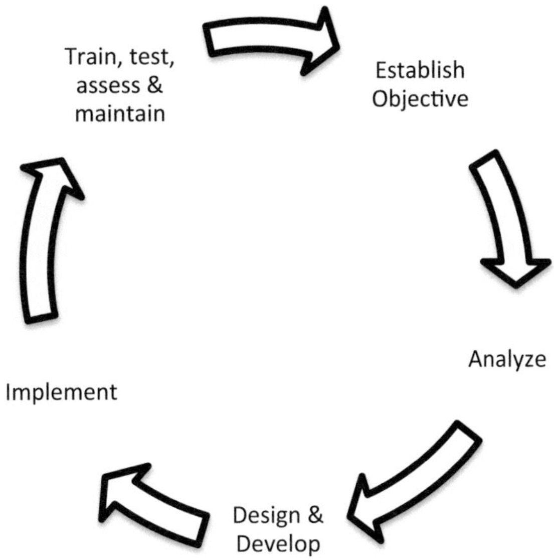

Fig. 2.2 Business continuity lifecycle

ii. Analyze
The first process of this stage is to gather all information regarding business processes, Infrastructure dependencies, data profiles, and frequency of using business infrastructure. The business impact analysis in terms of revenue and productivity loss due to service disruption is carried out. The critical business processes are identified and its recovery priorities are assigned. Risk analysis is performed for critical functions and its mitigation strategies are designed. The available BC options are evaluated using cost–benefit analysis.

iii. Design and develop
Teams are defined for various activities like emergency response, infrastructure recovery, damage assessment, and application recovery with clearly defined roles and responsibilities. Data protection strategies are designed and its required infrastructure and recovery sites are developed. Contingency procedures, emergency response procedures, recovery and restart procedures are developed.

iv. Implement
Risk mitigation procedures such as backup, replication, and resource management are implemented. Identified recovery sites are prepared to be used during disaster. Replication is implemented for every resource to avoid single point failure.

v. Train, test, assess and maintain
The employees who are responsible for BC maintenance are trained in all the proactive and reactive BC measures developed by the team. Vulnerability testing must be done to the BC plans for performance evaluation and limitation identification. Periodic BC plans updations are to be done based on the technology updation or business requirement modifications.

2.2.2 Information Availability

The ability of the traditional or cloud based IT infrastructure to perform its functionality as per the business expectation at the required time of operations is termed as *Information Availability* (IA). Accessibility, reliability, and timeliness are the attributes of IA. Accessibility refers to the access of information by the right person and at right time, reliability refers to the consistency and correctness of the information and timeliness refers to the time window during which the information will be available (Wiley 2010).

Information unavailability which is also termed as downtime leads to loss of productivity, loss of reputation, and loss of revenue. Reduced output per unit of labor, capital and equipment constitutes loss of productivity. Direct loss, future revenue loss, investment loss, compensatory payments, and billing loss are the various losses included in loss of revenue. Loss of reputation is the confidence loss or creditability loss with customers, suppliers, business partners, and bank (Somasundaram and Shrivastava 2009).

The sum of all losses incurred due to the service disruption is calculated using the metric, average cost of downtime per hour. It is used to measure the business impact of downtime and also assist to identify the BC solution to be adopted. The formula to calculate the average cost of downtime per hour is (Wiley 2010).

$$\mathrm{Avg}_{\mathrm{dt}} = \mathrm{Avg}_{\mathrm{pl}} + \mathrm{Avg}_{\mathrm{rl}}, \tag{2.1}$$

where

$\mathrm{Avg}_{\mathrm{dt}}$ is the "Average cost of downtime per hour"
$\mathrm{Avg}_{\mathrm{pl}}$ is the "Average productivity loss per hour"
$\mathrm{Avg}_{\mathrm{rl}}$ is the "Average revenue loss per hour"

The average productivity loss is calculated as

$$\mathrm{Avg}_{\mathrm{pl}} = \frac{\text{Total salary and financial benefits of all employees/week}}{\text{Average number of working hours per week}} \tag{2.2}$$

The average revenue loss per hour is calculated as

$$\mathrm{Avg}_{\mathrm{rl}} = \frac{\text{Total revenue of the organization per week}}{\text{Average number of working hours per week}} \tag{2.3}$$

IA is calculated as the time period during which the system was functional to perform its intended task. It is calculated in terms of system uptime and down time or in terms of Mean Time Between Failure (MTBF) and Mean Time to Recovery (MTTR).

$$\mathrm{IA} = \frac{\text{System uptime}}{(\text{System uptime} + \text{System down time})} \tag{2.4}$$

Table 2.1 Availability values and its permitted downtime

Availability %	Downtime %	Downtime per year	Down time per month	Down time per week
98	2	7.3 days	14.4 h	3.36 h
99	1	3.65 days	7.2 h	1.68 h
99.9	0.1	8.76 h	43.8 min	10.1 min
99.99	0.01	52.56 min	4.38 min	1.01 min
99.999	0.001	5.26 min	26.28 s	6.06 s

Or

$$IA = \frac{MTBF}{(MTBF + MTTR)} \tag{2.5}$$

The importance of IA is based on the exact timeliness requirement of the business operations and the same is used to decide the uptime specification. Sequence of "9 s" is used to indicate the uptime requirement based on which the allowed downtime for the service is also calculated. Table 2.1 lists out availability based uptime and down time specifications along with hours of downtime per week and per year (Somasundaram and Shrivastava 2009).

2.3 Traditional Software Reliability

Software is also a product that needs to be delivered with reliability tag attached. Profitability of software is directly related to achieving the precise objective of reliability. The software used in business is expected to adapt to the rapid changing business needs at a fast pace. Faster delivery time includes a tag "greater agility", which refers to the rapid response of the product to the changes in user needs or requirements (Musa 2004). Reliability of software gets influenced by either logical or physical failure. The bug that caused physical failure is corrected and the system is restored back to the state as it was before the appearance of bug. The bug that caused logical failure is removed and the system is enhanced.

Reliability/availability, rapid delivery and low cost are the most important characteristics of good software in the perspective of software users. Developing reliable software depends upon the application of quality attributes at each phase of the development cycle with main concentration on error prevention (Rosenberg et al. 1998). Various software quality attribute domain and its sub attributes are provided in Table 2.2.

As discussed in the above sections, reliability is user-oriented and it deals with the usage of the software rather than the design of the software. The evidence of reliability is obtained after prolonged running of the software. It relates operational experience with the influence of failures on that experience. Even though the reliability can be

Table 2.2 Software quality attribute domain and its attributes

Attribute domain	Attributes
Reliability	Consistency and precision
	Robustness
	Simplicity
	Traceability
	Correctness
Usability	Accuracy
	Clarity of documentation
	Conformity of operational environment
	Completeness
	Testability
	Efficiency
Adaptability	Modifiability or integrity
	Portability
	Expandability
Maintainability	Adaptability
	Modularity
	Readability
	Simplicity

obtained after operating it for a period of time, the consumers need software with some guaranteed reliability.

Well-developed reliability theories exists that can be applied directly for hardware components. The failure of hardware components occur due to design error failure, fabrication quality issues, momentary overload, aging, etc. The failure data are collected during the development as well as operational phase to predict the reliability of software. Major difference exists between the reliability measurements and metrics of hardware and software. The hardware reliability cannot be directly applied to software. Life of any hardware devices is classified into three phases such as burn-in, useful and burn-out. During the burn-in phase the failures are more as the product is in the nascent stage hence reliability is low. During useful phase the failure is almost constant as the product would have stabilized after all corrections. In the burn-out phase the product suffers from aging or wear-out issues and hence the failure will be high. This is represented in Fig. 2.3 as the popular bath tub curve. The same concept cannot be applied for software as there is not wear-out phase in software. The software becomes obsolete. Failure rate is high during the testing phase and the failure rate of software does not go down with age of the software. Figure 2.4 depicts the software reliability in terms of failure rate with respect to time. Software Reliability Engineering (SRE), a special field of engineering technique for developing and maintaining software systems.

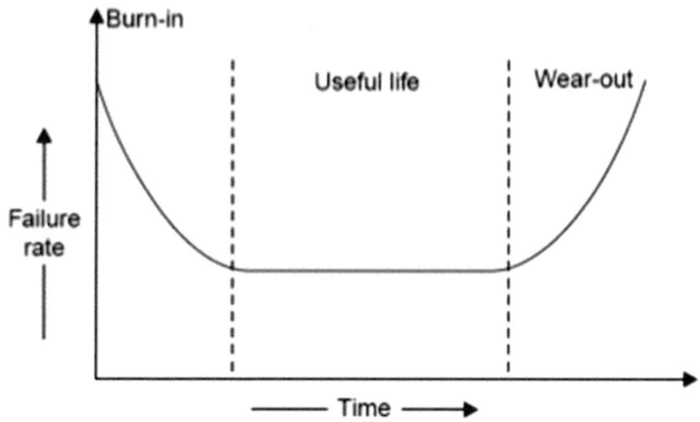

Fig. 2.3 Bath tub curve of hardware reliability

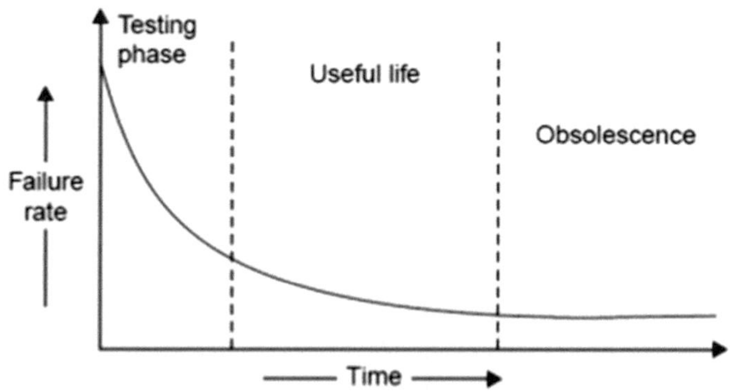

Fig. 2.4 Software reliability with respect to time

2.4 Reliability in Distributed Environments

Developments in communication technology and availability of cheap and powerful microprocessors have led to the development of distributed systems. Distributed system is software that facilitates execution of a program in multiple independent systems but gives an illusion as a single coherent system. These systems have more computing power sometimes even greater than mainframes. This helps in faster, enhanced and reliable execution of programs through load distribution. As the execution of a program is carried out by multiple systems, failure of a single system will be compensated by other systems in the distributed environment and hence these systems enjoy high resilience. Flexibility, enhanced communications, modular expandability, transparency, scalability, resource sharing, and data sharing are the benefits of these types of systems. World Wide Web (WWW) is an example of a biggest distributed system. These Distributed environments are preferred over

Table 2.3 Types of failures in distributed system

Type of failure	Reason for occurrence
Crash failure	Major hardware component or server crashes, leaving system unusable
Timing failure	System fails to respond to a request within particular amount of time
Omission failure	System fails to receive any incoming request and hence fails to send response to the client requests
Arbitrary failure	Server or a system sends arbitrary messages
Response failure	System sends incorrect massage as response to client's message

Table 2.4 Difference between faults in distributed system

Transient faults	Permanent faults
Occurrence will be for a short period	It is a permanent damage
It is hard to locate	It is easy to locate
Does not result in major system shutdown	Cause huge damage to the system performance
Examples are network fault, storage media fault or processor fault etc.	Example is an entire node level fault

traditional environments as they provide higher availability and high speed at low cost. Easy resource sharing and data exchange might cause concurrency and security issues. Various types of distributed systems are Distributed computing systems, Distributed information systems and Distributed pervasive systems

Faults in any component of distributed system results in failure. The failures thus encountered can lead to simple repairable errors or major system outage. Table 2.3 lists various failures of a distributed system.

Two general types of faults that occur in distributed systems are transient fault and permanent faults. Table 2.4 lists the difference between these two types of faults.

Apart from the above-mentioned general type of faults, various types of faults also occur in constituents of distributed systems such as components, processors and network. These faults are discussed as follows:

i. Component faults: These are faults that occur due to the malfunctioning or repair of components such as connectors, switches, or chips. These faults could be transient, intermittent or permanent. Transient faults are those that occur once and vanish with repetition of operations. Intermittent faults occur due to loose connections and keep occurring sporadically until the part is problem is fixed. Permanent faults results due to faulty or non-functional component. The system will not function until the part is replaced.
ii. Processor faults: The main component of a distributed system responsible of fast and efficient working is processor. Any faults in these processor functioning leads to three types of failures such as fail-silent, Byzantine and slowdown. In fail-silent failure the processor stops accepting input and giving output (i.e.) it stops functioning completely. Byzantine failure does not stop the processor working. The processor continues to work but it gives out wrong answers. In

slowdown failure, the faulty processor will function slowly and will be labeled as "Failed" by the system. These may return to normal and may issue orders leading to problems within the distributed system.

iii. Network faults: Network is the backbone of distributed systems. Any fault in network will lead to loss of communication. The failures that may arise are one-way link and network partition. In one-way link failure message transfer between two systems such as A and B will be in only one direction. For example, Assume system A can send message to system B but not receive reply back from it due to one-way failure. This will result in system A assuming that the other system B has failed. Network partition failure occurs due to the fault in the connection between two sections of systems. The two separated sections will continue working among them. When the partition fault is fixed, consistency error might occur if they had been working on the same resource independently during the network partition failure.

Designing a fault tolerant system with reliability, availability and security is essential to leverage the benefits of distributed systems. To ensure reliable communication between the processors, redundancy approach is incorporated in the design of a distributed system. Any one of the three types of redundancies such as information redundancy, time redundancy or physical redundancy can be followed to ensure continuous system availability. Information redundancy is addition of extra bits to the data to provide space for recovery from distorted bits. Time redundancy refers to the repetition of the failed communication or the transaction. This is the solution for transient and intermittent faults. Physical redundancy is the inclusion of new component in the place of failed component. The physical redundancy can be implemented as active replication, where each processor work will be replicated simultaneously. The number of replications depends on the fault tolerance requirement of the system. The other way of implementing physical redundancy is primary backup where along with the primary server an unused backup server will be maintained. Any outage in the primary server will initiate a switch for the backup server to be the primary server.

Check pointing technique can also be used to maintain continuity of the system. Process state, information of active registers and variables defines the state of a system at a particular moment. All these information about the system are collected and stored. These are called as checkpoints. The collection and storage process might occur as either user triggered, coordinated by process communication or message-based check pointing. When a system failure is encountered, the stored values are used to restore the system back to the recently stored check point level. This does have some loss of transaction details but eliminates the grueling process of repeating the entire application from the beginning. The check pointing method is useful but time consuming.

2.5 Defining Cloud Reliability

The demand for cost-effective and flexible scaling of resources has paved the way for adoption of cloud computing (Jhawar et al. 2013). Cloud computing industry is expanding day by day and Forrester had predicted that the market will grow from $146 billion in 2017 to $236 billion in 2020 (Bernheim 2018). It has also predicted growth in industry specific services offered by diverse pool of cloud service providers.

The reliability models of traditional software cannot be directly applied to cloud environment due to the technical shift from product oriented architecture to service oriented architecture. With the development in cloud computing, reliability of applications deployed on cloud attracts more attention of the cloud providers and consumers. The layered structure of cloud applications and services increases the complexity of its reliability process. Depending on the cloud services subscribed, the CSPs and the cloud consumer share the responsibility of offering a reliable service. Customer's trust on the services provided by CSP is paramount, particularly in case of SaaS service due to total dependency of business on the SaaS. Customers expect the services to be available all the time due to the advancement in cloud computing and online services (Microsoft 2014).

The main aim of applying the reliability concepts to cloud services is to

i. Maximize the service availability.
ii. Minimize the impact of service failure.
iii. Maximize the service performance and capacity.
iv. Enhance business continuity.

Reliability in terms of cloud environment is viewed to have failure tolerance, which is quantifiable, along with some of the qualitative features like adherence to the compliance standards, swift adaptability to the changing business needs, implementation of open standards, easy data migration policy and exit process etc. Various types of failures like request timeout failure, resource missing failure, overflow failure, network failure, database failure, software and hardware failures are interleaved in cloud computing environment (Dai et al. 2009).

The cloud customers and cloud providers share the responsibility for ensuring a reliable service or application when they enter into a contract agreement (SLA), either to utilize or to provide the cloud services. Depending on the cloud offering the intensity of responsibility varies for both of them. If it is an IaaS offering, then the customer is completely responsible for building a reliable software solution and the provide is responsible for providing reliable infrastructure such as storage, compute core or network. If it is a PaaS offering, then the provider is responsible for providing reliable infrastructure and OS and the customer is responsible for designing and installation of reliable software solution. If it is SaaS offering, then the provider is completely responsible for delivering a reliable software service at all the times of need and the customer has little or nothing to do for reliable SaaS (Microsoft 2014).

2.5.1 Existing Cloud Reliability Models

There are a number of models proposed by different researchers in the area of cloud computing environments. The areas of research are interleaved failures in cloud models, scheduling reliability, quality of cloud services, homomorphic encryption methods, multi state system based reliability assessment.

A cloud service reliability model based on Graph theory, Markov model and queue theory has been proposed on the basis that the failures in cloud computing models are interleaved by Dai et al. (2009). The parameters that are considered for this model are processing speed, amount of data transfer, bandwidth and failure rates. Graph theory and Bayesian approaches are integrated to develop an algorithm for evaluation.

Banerjee et al. (2011) have designed a practical approach to assess the reliability of the cloud computing suite using the log file details. Traditional reliability of the web servers are used as a base to provide availability and reliability of SaaS applications. The data are extracted from the log file using log filtering method based on transaction categorization and workload characteristics based on session and request counts. The transactions of the registered users are taken into consideration due to its direct business impact. Suggestions have been done to include the findings of the log based reliability techniques and measures as a component in the SLA.

Malik et al. (2012) have proposed the reliability assessment, fault tolerance, and reliability based scheduling model for PaaS and IaaS. Different reliability assessment algorithms for general, hard real time and soft real time applications are presented. The proposed model has many modules, Out of them; Fault monitor module is used to identify the faults during execution, Time checker module is used to identify the real time processes and the core module Reliability Assessor to assess the reliability of each compute instance. The algorithm proposed for general applications are more focused towards failure and more adaptive.

Dastjerdi and Buyya (2012) have proposed automation of the negotiation process between the cloud service requester and the provider for discovery of services, scaling, and monitoring. Reliability assessment of the cloud provider is also proposed. The objective of the automated negotiation process is to minimize the cost and maximize availability for the requester and maximize cost and minimize availability for the providers. The challenges addressed are the tracking of reliability offers given by the provider and balancing resource utilization. The research findings conclude that the simultaneous negotiations with multiple requesters will improve profits for the providers.

Quality of Reliability of cloud services is proposed by Wu et al. (2012). A layered composable system accounting architecture is proposed rather than analyzing from consumer end or provider end. S5 system accounting framework consisting of Service existence, Service capability, Service availability, Service usability and Service self-healing are identified as levels of QoR for cloud services. The primary aim of this research is to analyze past events, update the occurrence probability and to make predictions of failure.

Resource sharing, distributed, and multi-tenancy nature and virtualization are the main reason for the increased risks and vulnerabilities of cloud computing Ahamed et al. (2013). Public key infrastructure that includes confidence, authentication and privacy is identified as the base for providing essential security services that will eventually build trust and confidence between the provider and consumer. The challenges and vulnerabilities of the cloud environments are discussed. Traditional encryption is suggested as a solution to handle some of the challenges to an extent. Data-centric and homomorphic encryption methods are suggested as the suitable solutions for the cloud environment challenges.

Hendricks et al. (2013) have designed "CloudHealth", a global system to be accessed by the entire country for providing reliable cloud platform for healthcare community in the USA. The attributes such as high availability, global access, secure and compliant are mentioned as the prime attributes for a reliable SaaS health product. OpenNebula is used as the default monitoring system for host and VM monitoring and for balanced resource allocations and the add-on monitoring is done using Zenoss, a Linus-based monitoring system. Tests on the add-on monitoring system were done by creating a network failure on a VM, kernel panic in a VM and using simulated failure of the VM's host machine which were immediately identified and notified to the administrators.

Wu et al. (2013) have modeled reliability and performance of cloud service composition based on multiple state system theory which is suitable for those systems that are capable of accomplishing the task with partial performance or degraded performance. Traditional reliability models are found unfit for cloud services because of the assumption of component execution independence. The reliability of cloud application is mentioned as the success probability of performance rate matching the user requirement. A fast optimization algorithm based on UGF and GA working with little time consumption has been presented in the paper which will eliminate the risk of state space explosion.

A model to measure the software quality, QoS and security of SaaS applications is proposed by Pang and Li (2013). The proposed model includes separate perspective for customer and platform provider. An evaluation model has been proposed based on this which will evaluate and categorize the level of SaaS product as basic or standard or optimized or integrated. The security metrics included in the model are customer security, data security, network security, application security and management security. Quality of experience, quality of platform and quality of application are the metrics that are considered for QoS. The characteristics of quality in use model and product quality model of ISO/IEC 25010:2011 is utilized for software quality metrics. The metric to be met of four levels of SaaS are also listed.

Anjali et al. (2013) has identified the undetermined latency and no or less control of the computing nodes are the reasons for the failure in cloud computing and a fault tolerant model has been devised for the same. The model evaluates the reliability of the node and decides on inclusion or exclusion of the node. An Acceptor module is provided for each VM which tests them and identifies its efficiency. If the results of the tests are produced before the specified time it is then sent to the timer module. Reliability Assessor checks the reliability of each VM after every computing cycle.

The initial reliability is assumed as 100%. Maximum and minimum reliability limits are predefined and the VM with reliability less than minimum is removed. The decision maker node accepts the output list of reliable nodes from the reliability assessor module and selects the node with high reliability.

2.5.2 *Types of Cloud Service Failures*

In traditional software reliability, four main approaches to build reliable software systems are fault prevention, fault removal, fault tolerance, and fault forecasting. Cloud computing environments are distinguished from traditional distributed computing due to its massive scale of resource and service sharing. Various types of failure that might occur in cloud service delivery which affects its reliability are

i. Service request overflow
ii. Request timeout
iii. Resource missing
iv. Software/hardware failure
v. Database failure
vi. Network failure

i. Service request overflow
Cloud service requests are handled by various data centers. The request queue of each processing facility will have limitation in handling maximum number of requests. This is maintained to reduce the wait time for the new requests. When the queue is full and if a new job request arrives, then it will be dropped. The user will not get the service due to the occurrence of service request overflow failure. The job will be completed by assigning it to other processing facility.
ii. Request timeout
Each cloud service request has due time set by the service monitor or the user. The load balancer will ensure that the requests are processed without any delay. "Pull" or "Push" process used by the load balancer will ensure smooth execution of service requests. If the waiting time for a cloud service request goes beyond the due time, then request timeout failure occurs. These types of failed requests are removed from the queue as its waiting will affect the processing of other requests which will eventually deteriorate the throughput of the requests.
iii. Resource missing
In cloud environments all shared resources such as compute, network, data, or storage are registered, controlled, and managed by Resource Manager (Dai et al. 2009). The resources can be added or removed depending on the business requirement. It might happen so that the previously registered resources may no longer be required and hence removed. The removal must be done through Resource Manager, so that the registry entry will also be removed. If not done, the resource will not be available but the entry exists and thus leads to data resource missing failure.

iv. Software/hardware failure
This refers to the failures that might happen due to the faults in the software module that is run in the cloud environment. It is similar to the normal software failure that occurs in the traditional software usage. The hardware resources available in the data centers have optimal utilization due to its shared usage pattern. These devices need periodic maintenance and upgradation. If not done failures may crop up due to aging of devices which will lead to hardware failure.

v. Database failure
Database for the cloud-based program modules will be stored in the same data center as that of the program or in any other neighboring data center depending on the load available. If both program module and data are stored in the same place, then chances of database failure is near to null. If the data is stored in one location and the program is stored in another location then chances for database connection related failures such as connection request failure, data access failure or other timeout failures might occur due to the remote access issues.

vi. Network failure
This is the back bone of cloud environments without which no operation can be performed. The responsibility and accountability of ensuring better connectivity (i.e.) connectivity without failure lie with both the provider as well as the consumer. Any loss in connection will lead to disruption in business continuity which will lead to financial and reputation loss. Any physical or logical breakage of the communication channel will lead to network failure.

2.5.3 Reliability Perspective

The responsibility of maintaining reliable services is with the consumer as well as with the provider depending on the type of cloud services being used in the organization. Figure 2.5 lists various components or layers that exist in IT service delivery. The features mentioned in gray are the one that are controlled by CSP. For On-premise IT services, none of the component is grayed as the total control of reliable IT service delivery is the responsibility of the IT team of the organization. IaaS deployments have very few features in the hands of CSP whereas in SaaS deployments, the total control of the application lies with CSP. Hence, the responsibility of ensuring reliable usage of cloud services is shared between provider and consumer depending on the type of service chosen. High availability, security, customer service, backup and recovery plans are some of the attributes that are essential across all type of cloud services.

2.5.3.1 Infrastructure as a Service

In IaaS service model, the base for any application execution such as server, storage and network is provided by CSP. Organizations opt for IaaS to have scalability

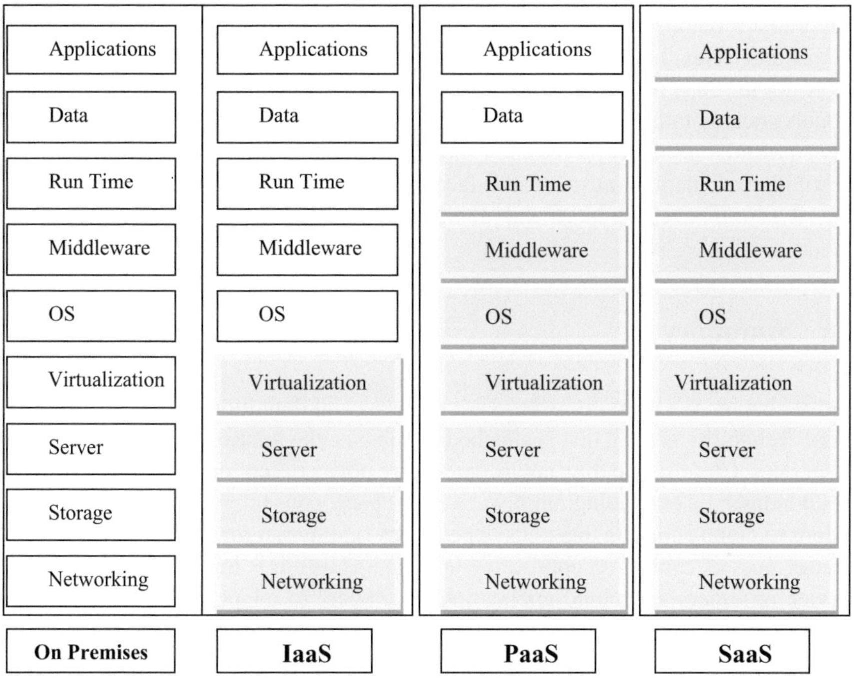

Fig. 2.5 Components of IT services

where resources can be provisioned and de-provisioned at the time of need. High availability, security, load balancing, storage options, location of data center, ability to scale resources and faster data access are essential attributes of any IaaS services.

2.5.3.2 Platform as a Service

PaaS service model are preferred by developers as they need not worry about installation and maintenance of servers, patches, authentication and upgrades. PaaS provides workflow and design tools, rich APIs to help in faster and easier application development. Hence, companies concentrate on enhancing user experience. Dynamic provisioning, manageability, performance, fault tolerance, accessibility and monitoring are the qualities that need to be taken care for maintaining reliability of PaaS environment.

2.5.3.3 Software as a Service

The reliability factors are considered from the requirement gathering phase till the delivery of software as a service. This type of service delivery requires more elaborated reliability factors identification. The responsibility of maintaining these factors lies with the provider as the consumer has little or no control on SaaS applications. SaaS reliability aspect has more importance than other service delivery models such as IaaS and PaaS. This is due to the fact that the business operations rely on it and it is mostly preferred by those who have less or no technical know-how. Reliability evaluation must include factors such as functionality of the software, security, compliance, support, and monitoring, etc.

2.6 Summary

In this chapter, we have discussed various terms and definitions pertaining to reliability. Reliability is a tag that is attached to enhance the trustworthiness of a product or services. Cloud computing environments are not an exception to this. Even though cloud industry is expanding rapidly at a faster pace, consumers are still having inhibitions to cloud adoption due to its dependency on Internet for working, remote data storage, loss of control on application and data. Hence it is imperative for all cloud service providers and cloud application developers to adopt all quality measures to provide efficient and reliable cloud services. The following chapters deal with outlining reliability factors and quantification methods for IaaS, PaaS, and SaaS.

References

Aggarwal, K. K., & Singh, Y. (2007). *Software engineering* (3rd ed). New Age International Publisher.

Ahamed, F., Shahrestani, S., & Ginige, A. (2013). Cloud computing: security and reliability issues. *Communications of the IBIMA, 2013,* 1.

Anjali, D. M., Sambare, A. S., & Zade, S. D. (2013). Fault tolerance model for reliable cloud computing. *International Journal on Recent and Innovation Trends in Computing and Communication, 1*(7), 600–603.

Banerjee, P., Friedrich, R., Bash, C., Goldsack, P., Huberman, B., Manley, J., et al. (2011). Everything as a service: Powering the new information economy. *IEEE Computer, Magazine, 3,* 36–43.

Bernheim, L. (2018). *IaaS vs. PaaS vs. SaaS cloud models (differences & examples).* Retrieved July, 2018 from https://www.hostingadvice.com/how-to/iaas-vs-paas-vs-saas/.

Briand L. (2010). *Introduction to software reliability estimation.* Simula research laboratory material. Retrieved May, 5, 2015 from www.uio.no/studier/emner/matnat/ifi/INF4290/v10/undervisningsmateriale/INF4290-SRE.pdf.

Dai, Y. S., Yang, B., Dongarra, J. & Zhang, G. (2009). Cloud service reliability: Modeling and analysis. In *15th IEEE Pacific rim international symposium on dependable computing* (pp. 1–17).

Dastjerdi, A. V., & Buyya, R. (2012). An autonomous reliability-aware negotiation strategy for cloud computing environments. In 12th IEEE/ACM international symposium on cluster, cloud and Grid computing (pp. 284–291).

Hendricks, E., Schooley, B., & Gao, C. (2013). Cloud health: developing a reliable cloud platform for healthcare applications. In *Conference proceedings of 3rd IEEE international workshop on consumer e-health platforms, services and applications* (pp. 887–890).

Jhawar, R., Piuri, V., & Santambrogio, M. (2013). Fault tolerance management in cloud computing: a system-level perspective. *IEEE Systems Journal* 7(2), 288–297

Lyu, M. R. (2007). Software reliability engineering: A roadmap. In *2007 Future of Software Engineering* (pp. 153–170). IEEE Computer Society.

Malik, S., Huet, F. and Caromel, D. (2012). Reliability Aware Scheduling in Cloud Computing. 7th IEEE International Conference for Internet Technology and Secured Transactions (ICITST 2012), 194–200.

Microsoft Corporation White paper. (2014). *An introduction to designing reliable cloud services*. Retrieved on September 10, 2014 from http://download.microsoft.com/download/.../An-introduction-to-designing-reliable-cloud-services-January-2014.pdf.

Musa, J. D. (2004). *Software reliability engineering* (2nd ed, pp. 2–3.). Tata McGraw-hill Edition.

Musa, J. D., Iannino, A., & Okumoto, K. (1990). Software reliability. *Advances in computers, 30,* 4–6.

Pang, X. W., & Li, D. (2013). Quality model for evaluating SaaS software. In *Proceedings of 4th IEEE international conference on emerging intelligent data and web technologies* (pp. 83–87).

Rosenberg, L., Hammer, T., & Shaw, J. (1998). Software metrics and reliability. In *9th international symposium on software reliability engineering*.

Somasundaram, G., & Shrivastava, A. (2009). *Information storage management*. EMC education services. Retrieved August 10, 2014 from www.mikeownage.com/mike/ebooks/Information%20Storage%20and%20Management.

Wiley, J. (2010). *Information storage and management: storing, managing, and protecting digital information*. USA: Wiley Publishing.

Wu, Z., Chu, N., & Su, P. (2012). Improving cloud service reliability—A system accounting approach. In *9th IEEE international conference on services computing (SCC)* (pp. 90–97).

Wu, Z., Xiong, N., Huang, Y., Gu, Q., Hu, C., Wu, Z., Hang, B. (2013). A fast optimization method for reliability and performance of cloud services composition application. *Journal of applied mathematics* (407267). Retrieved April, 2014 from http://dx.doi.org/10.1155/2013/407267.

Chapter 3
Reliability Metrics

Abbreviation

ISO	International Standards Organization
NIST	National Institute of Science and Technology
CSMIC	Cloud Service Measurement Index Consortium
SMI	Service Measurement Index
SOA	Service-Oriented Architecture
VM	Virtual Machines
CSP	Cloud Service Provider
VMM	Virtual Machine Manager

Reliability is equated to correctness of the products or services. A better way to ensure reliability is to identify various intermediate operational quality attributes or metrics instead of finding and fixing the issues or bugs. Cumulative computation of evaluated performance of quality attributes can be projected as overall reliability of the product or services. Working of Cloud services are based on Service-Oriented Architecture (SOA) and virtualization. SOA and cloud paradigm complements each other. Dynamic resource provisioning of cloud enhances SOA efficiency and services architecture of SOA helps cloud paradigm to enhance scalability and extensibility. Virtualization is a basic technology that runs cloud computing. Reliability aspects of SOA and virtualized environment are intertwined in the cloud reliability. Various organizations such as ISO, NIST and CSMIC have laid down recommendations for delivering reliable cloud services. These recommendations are considered as intermediate quality attributes and are converted as reliability metrics. The reliability metrics of Cloud computing environment varies with the type of service delivery model chosen. These metrics are further categorized based on the nature of its evaluation. Quantification of some metrics is done from the standards specification directly. Few of other metric quantifications are done based on the operational feedback from the existing customer while others are based on the expectations of the prospective customers versus actual working of the cloud services.

V. Kumar and R. Vidhyalakshmi, *Reliability Aspect of Cloud Computing Environment*, https://doi.org/10.1007/978-981-13-3023-0_3

3.1 Introduction

Reliability refers to the performance of the system as per the specification. Numerous components are involved in the performance of a system. Efficient working of these components as per expectation increases the overall efficiency of the system. It makes the system worthy enough to be trusted which in other words can be termed as it makes the system more reliable. The operations of these components thus become metric of reliability.

Some metrics are easy to calculate and thus are called quantitative metrics. Some metrics will have qualitative values like satisfactory level, adherence to compliance or not, security level expected with values like high, intermediate, and normal, etc. Both quantitative and qualitative metrics must be included in the final reliability evaluation to have holistic performance of the system. Hence it is important to device measures to quantify qualitative metrics. Role of metrics is essential to support informed decision making and can also be used for

i. Selecting the suitable cloud services
ii. Defining and enforcing service level agreements
iii. Monitoring the services rendered
iv. Accounting and auditing of the measured services

This chapter starts with reliability aspects of Service-Oriented Architecture (SOA) and virtualized environments. This is because these two are the backbone of cloud applications and services delivery.

SOA and cloud computing complements each other to achieve efficiency in service delivery. The working of cloud, SOA and its overlapping area between them is given in Fig. 3.1 (Raines 2009). Both of them share the basic concept of service orientation. In SOA, business functions are implemented as discoverable services and are published in the services directory. Users willing to implement the functionality have to request for the service and use them with the help of suitable standardized message passing facility. On the other hand, cloud computing provides all IT requirements as commodities that can be provisioned at the time of need from the cloud service providers. Both SOA and cloud relies on the network for execution of services. Cloud has broader coverage as it includes everything related to IT implementation whereas SOA is restricted only to software implementation concepts.

Virtualization is the basic technology that powers cloud computing paradigm. It is software that handles hardware manipulation efficiently, while cloud computing offers services which are results of this manipulation. Virtualization helps to separates compute environment from the physical infrastructure which allows simultaneous execution of multiple operating systems and applications. A workstation having Windows operating system installed can easily switch to perform task based on Mac without switching off the system. Virtualization has helped organizations to reduce IT costs and increase utilization, flexibility and efficiency of hardware.

Cloud computing had shifted the utilization of compute resources from asset based resources to virtual resources which are service based. Dependency of cloud implementations on SOA and virtualization makes it necessary to include discussion on

Cloud Computing	Common	SOA
• Resources provided as service • Utility Computing • On-demand provisioning • Data storage across cloud • Standards evolving for various services	• Network dependency • IP or wide area network supported service invocation • Integration using system of systems. • Producer / consumer Model	• Functionality as service. • Suitable for enterprise application integration • Consistency and integrity for services • Standardization between various module interactions.

Fig. 3.1 Similarities between cloud and SOA

these topics before deciding on the metrics of reliability. This chapter includes two separate sections that discuss about SOA and virtualization along with its reliability requirement concepts. Apart from this there are various standard organizations that work for setting the quality and performance standards for working of cloud computing. Organizations such as ISO, NIST, CSMIC, ISACA, CSA, etc., work for the betterment of cloud service development, deployment and delivery. These organizations had listed out various quality attribute that keeps updating depending on the technological changes. These quality features of ISO 9126, NIST specifications on cloud service delivery and Service Measurement Index (SMI) designed by CSMIC are discussed in detail. The chapter concludes with the categorization of the reliability metric along with its quantification mechanism. The metrics are classified based on the expectation, usage pattern and standard specification. Depending on the nature of the value stored in the metrics the quantification method varies.

3.2 Reliability of Service-Oriented Architecture

Software systems built for business operations need to be updated to keep pace with the ever changing global scope of business. Software architecture is chosen in a way to provide flexibility in system modification without affecting the current working and maintaining functional and non-functional quality attributes. This is essential for the success of these software systems. Use of Service-Oriented Architecture (SOA) helps to achieve flexibility and dynamism in software implementations. It provides adaptive and dynamic solutions for building distributed systems. SOA is defined in many ways by various companies. Some of them are

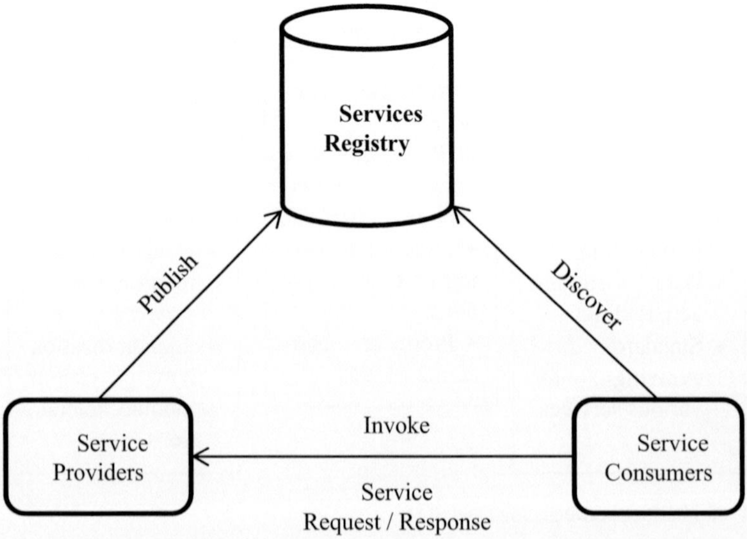

Fig. 3.2 Service oriented architecture (SOA)

"SOA is an application framework that takes business operations and breaks them into individual business functions and processes called services. SOA lets you build, deploy and integrate these services, independent of applications and the computing platform on which they run"—IBM Corporation.
"SOA is a set of components which can be invoked, and whose interface descriptions can be published"—Worldwide Web Consortium.
"SOA is an approach to organize information technology in which data, logic and infrastructure resources are accessed by routing messages between network interfaces"—Microsoft.

Service in SOA refers to complete implementation of a well-defined module of business functionality. These services are expected to have published interface that are easily discoverable. Figure 3.2 represents overall view of SOA.

Well-established services are further be used as blocks to build new business applications. The design principles of services are (Erl 2005; McGovern et al. 2003)

i. Services are self-contained and reusable.
ii. It logically represents a business activity with a specified outcome.
iii. It is a black box for users (i.e.) abstracts underlying logic.
iv. Services are loosely coupled.
v. Services are location transparent and have network-addressable interface.
vi. It may also consist of other services also.

Large systems are built using loose coupling of autonomous services which have the potential to bind dynamically and discover each other through standard protocols.

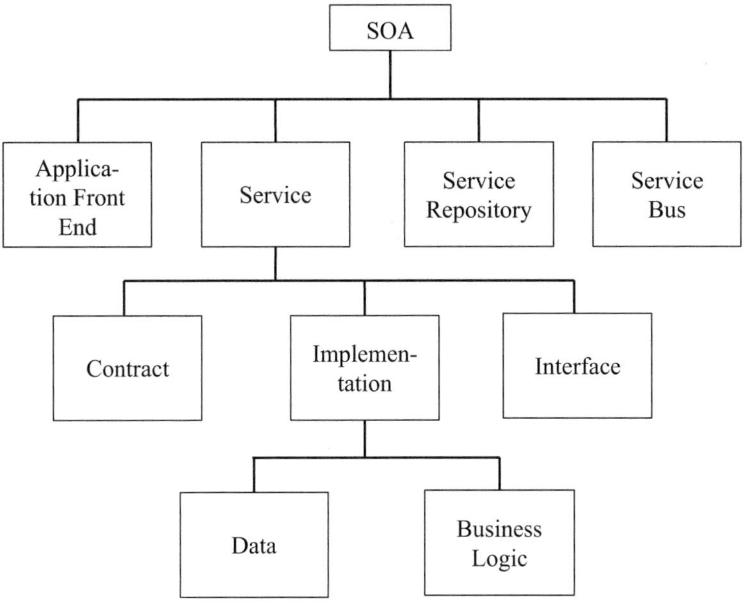

Fig. 3.3 Elements of SOA

This also includes easy integration of existing systems and rapid inclusion of new requirements (Arikan 2012).

Six core values of SOA are (innovativearchitects.com)

i. Business values are treated more than the technical strategy.
ii. Intrinsic interoperability is preferred over custom integration.
iii. Shared services are important over specific purpose implementation.
iv. Strategic goals are more preferred than project-specific benefits.
v. Flexibility has an edge over optimization.
vi. Evolutionary refinement is expected than initial perfection.

This style of architecture has reuse of services at macrolevel which help businesses to adapt quickly to the changing market condition in cost-effective way. This helps organizations to view problems in a holistic manner. In practicality, a mass of developers will be coding business operations in the language of their choice but complying with the standard with respect to usage interface, data and message communications. Figure 3.3 represents elements of SOA (Krafzig et al. 2005).

Various quality metrics that needs to be considered for ensuring effective and efficient SOA implementations are

i. Interoperability

Distributed systems are designed and developed using various platforms and languages. They are also used across various devices like handheld portable devices to mainframes. In early days of distributed systems introduction, there was no standard communication protocol or standard data formats to interoperate on global scale. The advent of frameworks such as Microsoft .Net, Sun's Java 2 Enterprise Edition (J2EE) and other open source alternatives like PHP, PERL, etc., have brought in standardization. Transparency in component communication is achieved through call-and-return mechanism. The interface format and the protocols required for communication is defined and the service implementation could be in any language or platform. To ensure the promise of cross-vendor and cross-platform interoperability, the Web Services-Interoperability Organization (WS-I) was formed in 2002. It publishes profiles that defines adherence to specific standards. These profiles are constantly being updated to cover all layers and standards of Web services stack (O'Brien et al. 2007).

ii. Availability and Usability

Availability refers to the ability of the service to be available at the time of need. In the SOA working scenario the service availability has to be viewed from the perspective of service users and that of the service providers. Non-availability of the service for the service users will bring dire consequences on the system and for the providers will affect their user base and revenue. SLA is signed between user and provider. It consists of details such as service guarantee level, escalation process and penalty details in case of failure to provide guaranteed services to users. Building contingency measures to maintain business continuity in case of service failure has to be done by the service users as risk mitigation measures.

Usability refers to the measure of user experience in handling services. Data communication between the service user and provider should have additional information like list valid inputs, list of alternatives for correct input, list of possible choices, etc. Services must also provide information related to placing service requests, canceling a placed request, providing aggregated data on service rendered, providing feedback for the ongoing services like percentage completed, expected time for completion, etc. (Bass and John 2003).

iii. Security

Confidentiality, authenticity, availability, and integrity are the main principles of security. Concern about security is inevitable in SOA due to its cross-platform and cross-vendor way of working. The following security measures for data are essential (O'Brien et al. 2007)

a. Text data in the messages must be encrypted to maintain privacy.
b. Trust on external providers must be ensured by proper authentication mechanism.
c. Access restriction based on user authorization must be provided.
d. Service discovery must be done after checking validity of the publishers.

The solutions for the service security issues are provided at the network infrastructure level. Digital certificates and Secure Socket Layers (SSLs) are used to provide encryption for data transmission and also to authenticate the communicating components. One of the main challenges in security is to maintain data integrity at time of service failure. This is because transaction management in distributed systems is very difficult due to the presence of loosely coupled components. Two-phase commit can be used which uses compatible transaction agents in the end points for interaction using standard formats.

iv. Scalability and Extensibility

Scalability refers to the ability of the SOA functions to change in size or volume based on the user needs but without any degradation in the existing performance. The options for solving capacity issues are horizontal scalability and vertical scalability. Horizontal scalability is the distribution of the extra load of work across computers. This might involve addition of extra tier of systems. Vertical scalability is the upgradation to more powerful hardware. Effective scaling increases the trust on the services.

Extensibility refers to the modification to the services capability without any affect to the existing parts of the services. This is an essential feature of SOA as this will enable software to adapt to the ever changing business needs. Loose coupling of the components enable SOA to perform the required changes without affecting other services. The restriction in the message interface makes it easy to read and understand but reduces extensibility. Tradeoff between interface message and extensibility is required in SOA.

v. Auditability

This is a quality factor which represents the ability of the services to comply with the regulatory compliance. Flexibility offered in the SOA design complicates the auditing process. End-to-end audit involving logging and reporting of distributed service requests are essential. This can be achieved by incorporating business-level metadata with each SOA message header such that it can be captured by the audit logs for future tracing. This implementation requires different service providers to follow messaging standards.

Reliability of SOA is based on the software architecture used for building services as the main focus is on components and data flow between them. Quality attributes mentioned above have to be followed to meet the SLA requirements. State-based, additive and path-based model are the three architecture based reliability models (Goýeva-Popstojanova et al. 2001). State-based reliability model uses control flow graph of the software architecture to estimate reliability. All possible execution paths are computed and the final reliability is evaluated for each path. Reliability of each component is evaluated and the total system reliability is computed as non-homogenous Poisson Process in additive model. Normal software reliability model cannot be directly used in SOA. This is because in SOA single software is built using interacting groups of autonomous services built by various geographically distributed stakeholders. These services collection might have varying levels of reliability assurance. The reliability of SOA must be evaluated for the basic components such as basic service working, data flow, service composition and complete work flow. As the service publication and discovery is done at run time, reliability model designed for SOA must react to runtime to evaluate the dynamic changes of the system.

Reliability of messages which are exchanged between services and reliability of the execution of the services are important for SOA reliability. Some of the issues that might occur in message passing are unreliable communication channel, connection break, failure to deliver messages, double delivery of the same message, etc. These issues are addressed by WS-Reliability (OASIS Consortium) and WS-Reliable Messaging (developed by Microsoft, IBM, TIBCO Software). Standard protocols are defined to ensure reliable and interoperable exchange of messages. Four basic assurances required are

i. In-order delivery—ensures the messages are delivered in the order it is sent.
ii. At least-once delivery—each message is delivered at least once.
iii. At-most-once delivery—no duplication of messages.
iv. Exactly once—each message is sent only once.

Service reliability refers to the operation of services as per specification or the ability of the service to report the service failures. Service reliability in SOA also depends on the provider of the service.

3.3 Reliability of Virtualized Environments

Virtualization is an old technique that had existed since 1960s but became popular with the advent of cloud computing. It is the creation of virtual (not actual) existence of server, desktop, storage, operating system, or network resources. It is the most essential platform that helps IT infrastructure of the organization to meet the dynamic business requirements. Implementation of virtualization assists IT organization to achieve highest level of application performance efficiency in cost effective manner. Organizations using vSphere with Operations Management of vmware have 30% increase in hardware savings, 34% increase in hardware capacity utilization and 36% increase in consolidation ratios (Vmware 2015).

Virtualization in cloud computing terms assists to run multiple operating systems and applications on the same server. It helps in creating the required level of customization, isolation, security, and manageability which are the basics for delivery of IT services on demand (Buyya et al. 2013). Adoption of virtualization will also increase resource utilization and this in turn helps to reduce cost. Virtual machines are created on the existing operating system and hardware. This provides an environment of logical separation from the underlying hardware. Figure 3.4 explains the concept of virtualization. Various types of virtualization are

i. Hardware virtualization

The software used for the implementation of virtualization is called Virtual Machine Manager (vmm) or hypervisor. In hardware virtualization the hypervisor will be installed directly on the hardware. It monitors and controls the working of memory, processor, and other hardware resources. It helps in the consolidation of various hardware segments or servers. Once the hardware systems are virtualized different

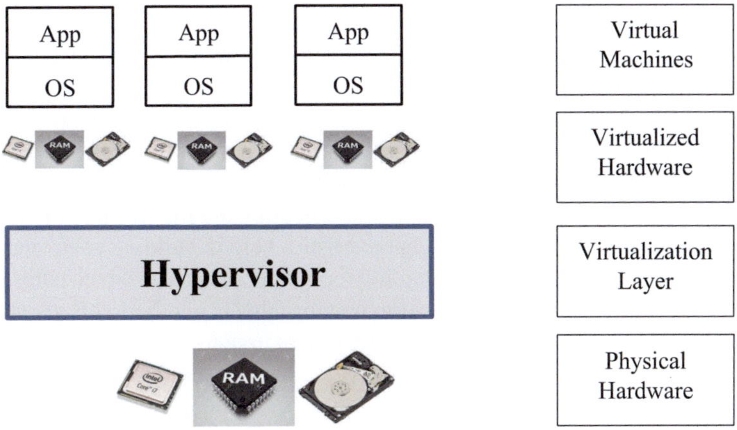

Fig. 3.4 Virtualization concepts

operating systems can be installed on the same machine with different applications running on them. The advantage of this type of virtualization is increased processing power due to maximized hardware utilization. The sub types of hardware virtualization are full virtualization, emulation virtualization, and paravirtualization.

ii. Storage virtualization

The process of grouping different physical storage into a single storage block with the help of networks is called as storage virtualization. It provides the benefit of using a single large contiguous memory without the actual presence of the same. This is type of virtualization is used mostly during backup and recovery processes where huge storage space is required. Advantages of this type of virtualization are homogenization of storage across devices of different capacity and speed, reduced downtime, enhanced load balancing and increased reliability. Block virtualization and file type virtualization are the sub-types of storage virtualization.

iii. Software virtualization

Installation of virtual machine software or virtual machine manager on the host operating system instead of installing on the machine directly is called as operating system virtualization. This is used in situations where testing of applications needs to be done on different operating systems platforms. It creates a full computer system and allows the guest operating system to run it. For example a user can run Android operating system on the machine installed with native OS as Windows OS. Application virtualization, Operating system virtualization and Service virtualization are the three flavors of software virtualization.

iv. Desktop virtualization

This is used as a common feature in almost all organizations. Desktop activities of the end users are stored in remote servers and the users can access the desktop from any location using any device. This enables employees to work conveniently at the comfort of their homes. The risk of data theft is minimized as the data transfer happens over secured protocols.

Hardware and software virtualizations are preferred the most with respect to cloud computing. Hardware virtualization is an enabling factor in Infrastructure as a Service (IaaS) and Platform as a Service (PaaS) is leveraged by software virtualization (Buyya et al. 2013). Managed isolation and execution are the two main reasons for virtualization inclusion. These two characteristics help in building controllable and secure computing environments. Portability is another advantage which helps in easy transfer of computing environments from one machine to another. This also helps to reduce migration costs. The motivating factors that urge to include virtualization are confidentiality, availability and integrity. There are achieved through properties like isolation, duplication and monitor.

Various quality attributes that needs to be maintained for assured reliability of virtualized environment are (Pearce et al. 2013)

i. Improved confidentiality

The efficiency of this quality attribute is achieved through effective isolation techniques. Placing OS inside virtual machines will help to achieve highest level of isolation. This will not only isolate software and the hardware of the same machine but also isolates various guest operating system and the hardware (Ormandy 2007). Proactive measures of intrusion and malware analysis processes are also simplified as they will be executed in virtualized environment and analyzed. This eliminates the full system setup for sample analysis. A fully virtualized system is set to offer an isolated environment but it has to be logically identical to physical environment.

ii. Duplication

Ability to capture all activities and restoring back at the time need is an important quality feature of virtual machines. Rapid capturing of the working state of the guest OS to a file is essential. The captured state is called as snapshot. The states of memory, hard disk, and other attached devices are captured in snapshot. The snapshots are captured periodically while running and also during any system outage. It is easy to restore previously captured snapshots. Sometimes snapshots are also restored while VMs are running with little degradation. The ability of VMs to store and restore states also provides hardware abstraction. This in turn improves the availability of virtual machines. Load balancing can be performed in VMs and is also referred a live migration.

iii. Monitor

The virtual machine manager has full control on the working of VMs. This also provides assurance that none of the VM activities will go unobserved. Full low-level visibility of the operations and the ability to intervene in the operations of the guest OS helps VM to capture, analyze and restore operations with ease (Pearce et al. 2013). The low-level visibility aspect of VM operations also referred to as *introspection* is useful for intrusion detection, software development, patch testing, malware detection, and analysis.

iv. Scalability

Scalable infrastructure with shared management is essential for efficient utilization of VM. Web-based virtual service management dashboard and interface is desirable which will help to enhance user experience of VM usage. The interface is also expected to have parameterized filtering and search facility along with Access Control List (ACL) feature for user or group management. This will help in easy provisioning and control of virtual environments.

v. Flexible usage and functionality

A virtualized environment is expected to support many protocol, message types and standards. Stateless/stateful/conditional/asynchronous operations are to be supported by virtualized services. Usage of reusable and shareable virtual components and the ability to learn and update environment dynamically with the service changes will help to improve flexibility. Dialog-based service creations, data-based function modeling along with simulation logging and preview facility will enable functionality coverage of virtualized environments.

3.4 Recommendations for Reliable Services

Standards organizations such as ISO/IEC, NIST, CSMIC, etc., have laid out various recommendations for providing cloud services. These are to be followed meticulously by the providers to claim that reliable services are being offered to customers. Compliance to these standards will also increase the trust factor and hence customer base will increase. Some of the standards that are to be followed with respect to cloud services are discussed below.

3.4.1 ISO 9126

This is an international standard that is used to evaluate software. Quality model, internal metrics, external metrics, and quality in use metrics are the four parts of this standard. Six quality characteristics identified by ISO 9126–1 are

i. Functionality

This refers to the basic purpose for which a product or service is designed. The complexity of functionality increases with the increase in functions provided by the software. The presence or absence of functionality will be marked by Boolean value. This represents the extent of relationship between overall business processes and software functionality.

ii. Reliability

After delivery of the software as per specification, reliability refers to the capability of the software to maintain its working under-defined condition for the mentioned period of time. This characteristic is used to measure the resiliency of the system. Fault tolerance measures should be in place to excel in resiliency.

iii. Usability

This feature refers to the ease of use of the system. It is connected with system functionality. This also includes learnability (i.e.) the ability of the end user to learn the system usage with ease. The overall user experience is judged in this and it is collected as a Boolean value. Either the feature is present or not present.

iv. Efficiency

This feature refers to the use of system resources while providing the required functionality. This deals with the processor usage, amount of storage utilized, network usage without congestion issue, efficient response time, etc. This feature has got close link with usability characteristics. The higher the efficiency the higher will be the usability.

v. Maintainability

This includes the ability of the system to fix the issues that might occur in the software usage. This characteristic is measured in terms of the ability to identify the faults and fixing it. This is also referred to as supportability. The effectiveness of this characteristic depends on the code readability and modularity used in the software design.

vi. Portability

The characteristic refers to the ability of the software to adopt with the ever changing implementation environment and business requirements. Including modularity by implementing object oriented design principles, separation logical design from the physical implementation will help to achieve adaptability without any affect to the existing system working.

Table 3.1 represents complete characteristics and sub-characteristics of ISO-9126-1 Quality Model (www.sqa.net/iso9126.html).

Understanding these quality attributes and incorporating them in the software design will enhance the quality of the software and its delivery. This will in turn enhance the overall trust on the software. Maintaining all quality attributes at its high efficient level is a challenging task. For example, if code is highly modularized then it is easy to maintain and also will have high adaptability. But this will have degradation in resource usage such as CPU usage. Hence, tradeoff needs to be applied wherever required depending on the business requirements of the customers. These quality attributes can also be considered as the metrics for the evaluation of software.

Table 3.1 ISO 9126-1 quality model characteristics

Characteristics	Sub-characteristics
Functionality	Accurateness (correctness of the function as per specification)
	Suitability (matching of business processes with software functionality)
	Compliance (maintaining standards pertaining to certain industry or government)
	Interoperability (ability of the software to interact with other software components)
	Security (protection from unauthorized access and attacks)
Reliability	Maturity (related to frequency to failure. Less frequency will indicate more maturity)
	Fault tolerance (ability of the system to withstand component or software failure)
	Recoverability (ability of the system to regain back from failure without any data loss)
Usability	Learnability (support for different level of learning users such as novice, casual and expert)
	Understandability (ease with the system working can be understood)
	Operability (ability of the software to be operated easily with few demo sessions)
Efficiency	Resource behavior (efficient usage of resources such as memory, CPU, storage and network)
	Time behavior (the response time for given operation e.g. transaction rate)
Maintainability	Changeability (amount of effort put into modify the system)
	Stability (ability of the system to change without affecting current working)
	Analyzability (log facility of the system which helps to analyze the root cause for failure)
	Testability (ability to test the system after each change implementation)
Portability	Adaptability (refers to the dynamism with which the system changes to the needs)
	Conformance (portability of the system with respect to data transfer)
	Installability (refers to the easy installation feature of the system)
	Attractiveness (the capability of the software to be liked by many users)
	Replaceability (plug-and play aspect of the software for easy updation of the system)

3.4.2 NIST

Migration to cloud must be preceded with an elaborated decision making process to identify a reliable cloud product or services. NIST had proposed Cloud Service Metric (CSM) model for evaluation of cloud product or services. This was initiated as there was a lack of common process to define cloud service measurements. It presents concrete metric definition which helps to understand rules and parameters to be used for the metric evaluation (NIST 2015). Metrology—a science of measurement is used in cloud computing for measurement of properties cloud services and also to gain common basic understanding of the properties. The relationship between properties and metrics is represented in Fig. 3.5. Understanding of the properties of cloud services is achieved through metrics. This will help to determine the service capabilities. For example, performance property of cloud product can be measured using one of the metric as response time. Metrics provide knowledge about aspects of the property through its expression, unit, and rules which can collectively be called as definition. It also provides necessary information for verification between observation and measured results (NIST 2015).

Converting property as metrics will help providers to show measurable properties for their products and services. This will also help customers and providers to agree on what will be rendered as services and cross verification on actuals that are rendered.

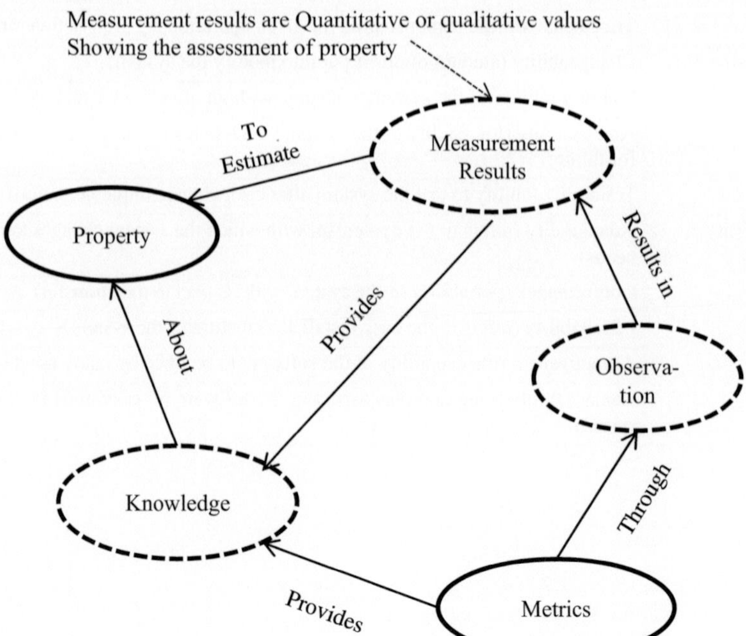

Fig. 3.5 Relation between property and metrics

For example availability is mentioned in terms of percentage like 99.9, 99.99%, etc. These are converted into amount of downtime and can be checked with the actual downtime that was encountered.

Metrics used in cloud computing service provisioning can be categorized as service selection, service agreement, and service verification.

i. Metrics for service selection

Service selection metrics are used for identifying and finalizing the cloud offering that is best suitable for business requirement. Independent auditing or monitoring agencies can be used to produce metrics values such as scalability, performance, responsiveness, availability, etc. These values can be used by the customers to assess the readiness and the service quality of the cloud provider. Some of the metrics like security, accessibility, customer support, and adaptability of the system can be determined from the customers who are currently using the cloud product or services.

ii. Metrics for service agreement

Service Agreement (SA) is the one that binds the customer and provider in a contract. It is a combination of Service Level Agreement (SLA) and Service Level Objective (SLO). It sets the boundaries and allowed margin of error to be followed by providers. It includes terms definition, service description, and roles and responsibilities of both provider and customer. Details of measuring cloud services like performance level and the metric used for monitoring and balancing is also included in SLA.

iii. Metrics for service measurement

This is designed with the aim to measure the assurance of meeting service level objectives. In case of failure to meet the guaranteed service levels, pre-determined remedies has to be initiated. Metrics like notification of failure, availability, updation frequency, etc., had to be check. These details are gathered from the dash board of the product or services or accepted as feedback from the existing users.

Other aspects of cloud usage can also be measured using metrics for auditing, accounting, and security. Accounting is linked with the amount of usage of service. Auditing and security is related with assessing of compliance for certification requirement related to the customer segment. Figure 3.6 represents various property or functions that are required for management services offered. These are broadly classified as business support, portability and provisioning (Liu et al. 2011).

3.4.3 CSMIC

Cloud Service Measurement Index Consortium (CSMIC) has developed Service Measurement Index (SMI). It is a set of business related Key Performance Indicators (KPIs), which will provide standardized method for comparing and measuring cloud based business services. SMI has a hierarchical framework with seven top-level

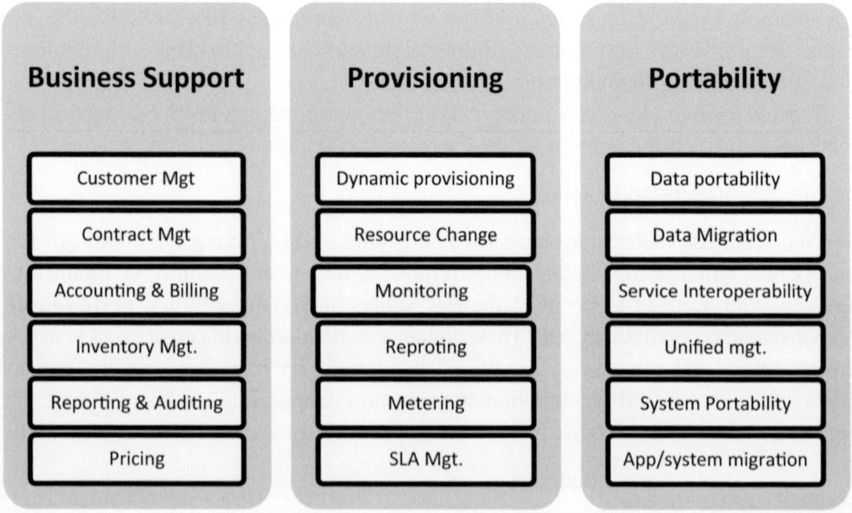

Fig. 3.6 Cloud services management

Table 3.2 Sub attributes of *accountability*

Sub attribute	Description
Auditability	Facility to be provided to customers for verification of the adherence to standards and processes
Compliance	Possession of various valid certificates to prove adherence to standards
Contracting experience	Ability to retrieve details about service quality from the existing clients
Sustainability	Provide proof for the usage of renewable energy resources to protect society and environment
Provider Support	Extent to which the assistance is provided to clients in times of service unavailability or usage issues
Ethicality	The manner in which business practices and ethics are followed. The manner in which the provider conducts business

categories which are further divided into sub categories. First level quality attributes are (CSMIC 2014)

i. Accountability

Evaluation of this attribute will help customers to decide about the trust factor on the provider. The attributes are related to the organization of the cloud service provider. Various sub attributes of *accountability* is given in Table 3.2.

Table 3.3 Sub attributes of *agility*

Sub attribute	Description
Adaptability	Ability of the cloud services to change based on the business requirements of the clients
Elasticity	Ability of the cloud services to adjust the resource consumption with minimal or no delay
Flexibility	Ability of the cloud products or services to include or exclude features as per client requirement
Portability	Ability to migrate existing on-premise data or ability migrate from one provider to another
Scalability	Ability to increase or decrease resource provisioning as per the client requirements

Table 3.4 Sub attributes of *assurance*

Sub attribute	Description
Availability	Presence of service availability windows as per the SLA specification
Maintainability	Ability of the cloud products or services to keep up with the recent technology changes
Recoverability	Rate at which the services return back to normalcy after unplanned disruption
Reliability	Ability to render services without any failure under given condition for a specified period of time
Resiliency	Ability of the system to perform even in times of failure with one or two components

ii. Agility

This attribute will help customers to identify the ability of the provider to meet the changing business demands. The disruption due to product or service changes is expected to be minimal. Table 3.3 lists the sub attributes of *agility*.

iii. Assurance

This attribute will provide the likelihood of the provider to meet the assured service levels. Sub attributes of *assurance* are listed in Table 3.4.

iv. Financial

Evaluation of this attribute will help customers to prepare cost benefit analysis for cloud product or service adoption. It will provide an idea about the cost involved and billing process. The sub attributes are billing process and cost. Billing process will provide details about the period of interval at which the bill will be generated. Cost will provide details about the transition cost, recurring cost, service usage cost, and termination cost.

Table 3.5 Sub attributes of *performance*

Sub attribute	Description
Functionality	Providing product or service features in tune with the business processes
Accuracy	The correctness with which the services are rendered as per SLA specification
Suitability	The extent to which the product features match with the business requirements
Interoperability	Extent to which the services easily interact with services of other providers
Response time	The measurement of time within which the service requests are answered

Table 3.6 Sub attributes of *security and privacy*

Sub attribute	Description
Security management	Capability of the provider to ensure safety to client data by possessing various security certificates
Vulnerability management	Holding mechanism to ensure services are protected from recurring and new evolving threats
Data integrity	Maintaining the client data as it was created and stored. It shows data is accurate and valid
Privilege management	Existence of policies and procedures to ensure that only authorized personnel access the data
Data location	Facility provided to the clients to restrict data storage location

v. Performance

Evaluation of this attribute will prove the efficiency of the cloud product or services. Sub attributes of *performance* are listed in Table 3.5.

vi. Security and privacy

This attribute will help customers to have a check on the safety and privacy measures followed by the provider. It also indicates the level of control maintained by the provider for service access, service data. and physical security. Table 3.6 lists various sub-attributes of *security and privacy* attribute.

vii. Usability

This attribute is used to evaluate the ease with which the cloud products can be installed and used. Sub-attributes of usability are listed in Table 3.7.

All the above-mentioned quality attributes of ISO 9126, NIST and CSMIC are updated periodically based on the changing technology and growing business adoption of cloud. These quality attributes have been taken into consideration and the reliability metrics are designed. This is done with the basic idea that entire reliability of the product can be enhanced if the intermediate operations are maintained of high quality. The reliability metrics of three cloud services, IaaS, PaaS and SaaS are explained in detail in the next chapter.

Table 3.7 Sub attributes of *usability*

Sub attribute	Description
Accessibility	Degree to which the services are utilized by the clients
Installability	The time and effort that is required by the client to make the services up and running
Learnability	Measure of time and manpower required to learn about the working of the product or services
Transparency	Ability of the system which makes it easy for the clients to understand the change in features and its impact on usability
Understandability	The measure of ease with which the system functions and it relation to business process can be understood

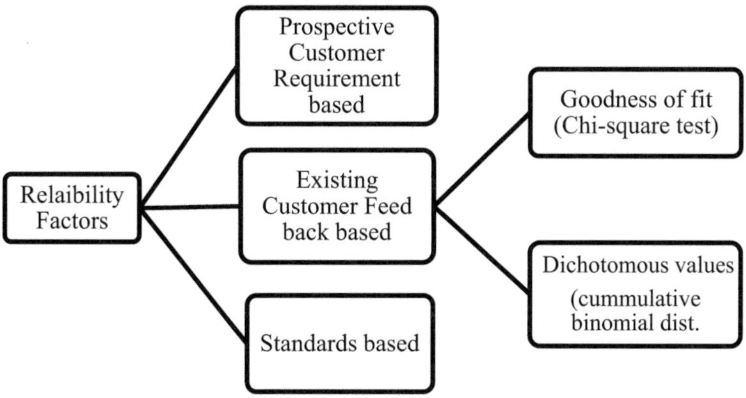

Fig. 3.7 Categorization of reliability metrics

3.5 Categories of Cloud Reliability Metrics

The metrics used for cloud reliability calculations are the quality attributes of the products. These metrics are defined in detail in the next chapter. Some of them are quantitative while few others are qualitative. The qualitative metrics are also gathered through questionnaire mechanism and are quantified. Metric evaluation of both the types is based on various calculations methods. The three major classifications used in this book are

i. Expectation-based
ii. Usage-based
iii. Standards-based.

Figure 3.7 illustrates the categorization of reliability metrics used in the following chapters. These are also named as Type I, Type II, and Type III metrics.

3.5.1 Expectation Based Metrics

These are also referred to as Type I metrics. These metrics are computed based on the input from prospective customers. These are the customers who are willing to adopt cloud services for business operations. Input for Type I metrics has to be provided by the end user of the organization. End users providing input to Type I metrics should possess the following:

1. Clear understanding of the business operations
2. Knowledge about cloud product and services
3. List of modules that need to be moved to cloud platform
4. Amount of data that need to be migrated
5. Details of on-premise modules that has to interoperate with cloud products
6. Security and compliance requirements
7. Risk mitigation measures expected from cloud services
8. List of data center location choices (if any)

Prospective customers will approach the proposed reliability evaluation model with a collection of shortlisted cloud products or services. The model will assist them to choose the cloud product that suits their business needs with the help of above inputs provided by them.

The customer requirements based on the above-listed points are accepted using a questionnaire.[1] The business requirements of the prospective customer are checked against actual offerings of the SaaS product. The formula to be used for this checking is

$$\frac{\text{Number of features offered by the product}}{\text{Total number of features required by the customer}} \tag{3.1}$$

Based on this calculation, the success probability of the product is measured. The inclusion of this type of factor enhances the customer orientation of the proposed model.

Example 3.1

If a customer expects 10 features to be present on a product or services and out of it 8 is being offered by the provider, then the probability value of 8/10 = 0.8 is the reliability value.

3.5.2 Usage Based Metrics

This metrics is also referred to as Type II metrics. These metrics provide an insight into the reliability of the service provided by checking the conformance of the services

[1]Detailed questionnaire is listed in Chap. 5.

assured. The rendered services are compared with that of the guaranteed and based on this comparison the reliability values are computed. The product usage experiences of the existing customer are gathered using questionnaire. This will be the actual working details of the cloud products. The assured working details are gathered from the product catalog. These are compared using on the following ways to calculate probability of the cloud products or services. Based on the nature of value gathered, either

Chi-square test or binomial distribution method or simple division method is used to identify the reliability of the metric.

i. Chi-square test

Chi-square test is used with two types of data. One is used with quantitative values to check goodness of fit to determine whether the sample data matches with the population. The other test is used with categorical values to test for independence. In this type of test two variables are compared for relation using contingency table. In both the tests, higher chi-square value indicates that sample does not match with population or there is no relation. Lower chi-square value indicates that sample matches population or there is relation between the values.

In this book, chi-square test method is used to when the assured value for rendering services are numeric. Example assured updation frequency, availability, mirroring latency, backup frequency, etc. The expected values for these metrics are retrieved from SLA and the observed values of these are accepted from the existing customers. Computations between observed and expected values are performed and goodness of fit of the observed value with that of the assured value is used to compute the final reliability of the metric. The null hypothesis and the alternative hypothesis for Chi-square test is taken as

$$\text{Null hypothesis } H_o = \text{Observed value} = \text{Assured value}$$
$$\text{Alternate hypothesis} = H_A = \text{Observed value} \neq \text{Assured value}$$

The Chi-square value χ^2 is calculated using formula

$$\chi^2 = \sum_{i=1}^{n} \frac{(O_i - E_i)^2}{E_i} \tag{3.2}$$

Smaller Chi-square statistics value χ^2 indicates the acceptance of null hypothesis (i.e.) service renders as per SLA assurance and the large χ^2 value indicates the rejection of null hypothesis, i.e., service not rendered as per assurance. Based on the χ^2 value, the goodness of fit will be identified. Based on this value the chance probability is calculated, which is used as the reliability value. The degree of freedom is used for chance probability calculations. Degree of freedom is the number of customers surveyed − 1. (Detailed discussion about degree of freedom is beyond the scope of this book). If the χ^2 value is 0 it indicates that observed and assured values are the same, then the chance probability is 1.

Table 3.8 Score of syndicates

Syndicate number	Observed average score
1	69
2	86
3	72
4	93
5	75
6	90
7	72
8	88
9	73
10	93
11	70
12	95

Example 3.2

Let us take the example of mark prediction and actual marks earned in the exam. A course had 120 students and they are divided into 12 syndicates comprising of 10 students in each syndicate. The odd number syndicates were assigned to class A, and even number syndicate is assigned to class B. Class test was conducted in statistics. Based on the interaction and caliber assessment, the tutor had predicted that the average score of class B will score 90 marks and that of class A will score 75. Table 3.8 lists the actual average scores of the class test. Conduct chi-square test to check the accuracy of tutor's prediction.

Tutor prediction for Class B is 90 and that of Class A is 75. Hence syndicate 1, 3, 5, 7, 9, 11 will have expected value as 75 and syndicate 2, 4, 6, 8, 10 and 12 will have expected value as 90. Table 3.9 shows calculations for χ^2.

The sum of the last column in the above Table 3.9 is 1.80667. This is the χ^2 value. Small χ^2 value indicates that the teacher prediction is correct. It matches with the actual scores of the students of both the sections.

ii. Binomial distribution

The results of experiments that have dichotomous values "success" or "failure" where the probability of success and failure is the same with every time of experiment is called as Bernoulli trials or binomial trials. Examples of binomial distribution usage in real life can be for drug testing. Assume a new drug is introduced in the market for curing some diseases. It will either cure the disease which is termed as "success" or it will not cure which is termed as "Failure".

This is used to evaluate metrics values which indicate the success in rendering the assured services or the failure in meeting the SLA specification. The reliability of this type of value is calculated using binomial distribution function. This value will indicate whether the services were rendered or not. Examples are audit log success, log retention, recovery success, etc., the formula to calculate the probability of success is

$$f(x) = \binom{n}{x} p^x q^{n-x}, \tag{3.3}$$

where

n	is the number of trials
x	indicates the count of success trials
$n-x$	indicates the count of failed trials
p	is the success probability
q	is the failure probability
$f(x)$	is the probability of obtaining exactly x good trials and $n-x$ failed trials

The value mentioned as $\binom{n}{x}$ is ${}_nC_x$ which is calculated as $n!/((n-x)! * x!)$

The average value of the binomial distribution is used to obtain the reliability of the provider in meeting the SLA specification.

$$F(x) = \frac{\sum_{r=0}^{n} f(r)}{n} \tag{3.4}$$

Example 3.3

A coin is tossed 10 times. What is the probability of getting six heads? The probability of getting heads and tails are the same, which means it is (0.5).

The number of trails n is 10.

The odds of success, which indicates the value of p is 0.5.

The value of q is $(1-p)$ which is 0.5.

The number of success (i.e.) x is 6

Table 3.9 Sample chi-square test calculation

Syndicate	Observed (O_i)	Expected (E_i)	$(O_i - E_i)$^2	$(O_i - E_i)$^2/E_i
1	69	75	36	0.48
2	86	90	16	0.177778
3	72	75	9	0.12
4	93	90	9	0.1
5	75	75	0	0
6	90	90	0	0
7	72	75	9	0.12
8	88	90	4	0.044444
9	73	75	4	0.053333
10	93	90	9	0.1
11	70	75	25	0.333333
12	95	90	25	0.277778

$$P(X = 6) = {}_{10}C_6 * 0.5 \wedge 6 * 0.5 \wedge (10 - 6)$$
$${}_{10}C_6 = 10!/((10 - 6)! * 6!) = 210$$
$$0.5 \wedge 6 = 0.015625$$
$$0.5 \wedge 4 = 0.0625$$
$$P(x = 6) = 210 * 0.015625 * 0.0625 = 0.205078125$$

The probability of getting head six times when a dice is thrown 10 times is 0.205078125.

iii. Simple division method

Some of the features like response and resolution time for trouble shooting, notification or incidence reporting will be guaranteed in the SLA. The providers will keep claims like there will be immediate resolution to issues, all downtime and attacks will be reported, etc. Numeric value for these types of claims will not be guaranteed in the SLA. In such cases the simple division method is used for metric evaluation. It is the simple probability calculations based on number of sub events and total occurrence of the event. The formula used is

$$\frac{\text{Number of times events has happened as per assurance}}{\text{Total number of occurence of the event}} \tag{3.5}$$

Example 3.4

Assume a car company selling used cars has assured to provide free service for 1 and ½ year with the duration of three month between each service. In a span of 18 months the company should provide six services. This is the assured value calculated from the company statement. The company also claims to have a good customer support and after sales service system. Free service reminders will be sent a week prior to the scheduled service date through call and also through mail. The reality of the service notification reminders provided is accepted from the owner of the car. If the owner gets service reminders before each service it is counted as success and if they do not it is counted as failure.

If the customer tells all six services were provided and notifications were given a week prior to the scheduled service then success value is 6. The reliability of the company for rendering prior service notification is 1 (6 assured and 6 provided so 6/6 = 1).

If the customer says that all six free services were given but got reminder call only for five services, then the reliability of the company for rendering prior service notification is 5/6 = 0.83.

3.5.3 Standards-Based Metrics

This type of metrics also referred to as Type III metrics is used to measure the adherence of the product to the standards specified. Due to the cross border and globally distributed working of cloud, various standards are required to be maintained depending on the country in which it is used. Various organizations such as CSA, ISO/IEC, CSCC, AICPA, CSMIC, and ISACA are working towards setting the standards for cloud service delivery, data privacy and security, data encryption policies, and other service organization controls (www.nist.gov). It is not mandatory for the CSP to acquire all available cloud standards. The standards are to be maintained depending on the type of customers for whom the cloud services are being delivered. Conformance to these standards increases the customer base of the CSP as this eventually increases the trust of the CC on the CSP. The conformance to the standards is revealed by acquiring certificates of standards. These certificates are issued after successful auditing process and have validity included. Possession of valid certificate is essential which will reflect the strict standards conformance. The quality standards are amended periodically depending on the technology advancements. The CSP are expected to keep updated with the new emerging quality standards and include them appropriately in their service delivery.

The basic requirements of the standards designed by International Standards Organizations, which are maintained in the repository layer of the model requires updations depending on the quality standard amendments. A subscription to these standards sites will provide alerts on the modification of the existing standards and inclusion of the new standards. This is used as a reminder to perform standards repository updation process.

These are checked against the features offered by the product. The checking is done using the formula

$$\frac{\text{Number of standards certificates possed by the organization}}{\text{Number of certificates suggested by the standards}} \tag{5.2}$$

Based on their valid certificate possession the success probability of the competency to match the standards requirements is measured.

Example 3.5

Every business establishment need to have the required certifications to comply with the government rules and regulations. Possession of these certifications will also help providers to gain trust of the customers.

Assume a vendor supplies spices and grains to chain of restaurants. The vendor should possess all certificates related to food safety and standards. If the vendor is in India then company must possess FSSAI (Food Safety and Standards Authority License), Health/Trade license, company registrations, etc. Set of required licenses vary from country to country. Apart from this it is also dependent on the place and industry, for which the services or products are provided.

If the grain supplier is expected to have five certificates and all five are possessed by the vendor then the metric of certificate possession will have the value 1 (5/5). If the grain supplier has only three out of five required certificates, then the metric value will be $3/5 = 0.60$.

3.6 Summary

This chapter has detailed the need of metrics, use of SOA and virtualization in cloud service delivery and various standards followed in cloud service delivery. SOA complements cloud usage and cloud implementation enhances flexibility of SOA implementation. Based on this the reliability requirements of SOA are also discussed in detail. Virtualization is the backbone of cloud deployments as it helps in efficient resource utilization and cost reduction. The reliability aspects of virtualization are discussed as it will be the base for IaaS reliability metrics. Various quality requirements suggested by organizations like ISO 9126, NIST, and CSMIC are discussed in detail. The reliability metrics to be discussed in the next chapter are derived from these quality features. The chapter concludes with the classification of the metric types. All reliability metrics value will not be of same data type. They will be of numeric or Boolean. The values will be either quantitative or qualitative. Some of the metrics can be calculated directly from the product catalog, while others need to be calculated based on the feedback accepted from the existing users. The categorizations are done as expectation-based (Type I), usage-based (Type II), and standards-based (Type III). The mathematical way of metric calculation is also explained with examples.

References

Arikan, S. (2012, September). Automatic reliability management in SOA-based critical systems. In *European conference on service-oriented and cloud computing*.

Bass, L., & John, B. E. (2003). Linking usability to software architecture patterns through general scenarios. *Journal of Systems and Software, 66*(3), 187–197.

Buyya, R., Vecchiola, C., & Selvi, S. T. (2013). *Mastering cloud computing: Foundations and applications programming*. McGraw Hill Publication.

CSMIC. (2014, July). *Service measurement index framework versions 2.1*. Retrieved July, 2015 from http://csmic.org/downloads/SMI_Overview_TwoPointOne.pdf.

Erl, T. (2005, April). *A look ahead to the service-oriented world: Defining SOA when there's no single, official definition*. Retrieved May, 2014 from http://weblogic.sys-con.com/read/48928.htm.

Goýeva-Popstojanova, K., Mathur, A., & Trivedi, K. (2001, November). Many architecture-based software reliability models. Comparison of architecture-based software reliability models. In *ISSRE* (p. 22). IEEE.

Krafzig, D., Banke, K., & Slama, D. (2005). *Enterprise SOA: Service-oriented architecture best practices*. Prentice Hall Professional.

Liu, F., Tong, J., Mao, J., Bohn, R., Messina, J., Badger, L., et al. (2011). NIST cloud computing reference architecture. *NIST Special Publication, 500*(2011), 292.

McGovern, James, Tyagi, Sameer, Stevens, Michael, & Matthew, Sunil. (2003). *Java web services architecture*. San Francisco, CA: Morgan Kaufmann Publishers.

NIST Special Publication Article. (2015). Cloud computing service metrics description. An article published by NIST Cloud Computing Reference Architecture and Taxonomy Working Group. Retrieved September 12, 2016 from http://dx.doi.org/10.6028/NIST.SP.307.

O'Brien, L., Merson, P., & Bass, L. (2007, May). Quality attributes for service-oriented architectures. In *Proceedings of the international workshop on systems development in SOA environments* (p. 3). IEEE Computer Society.

Ormandy, T. (2007). An empirical study into the security exposure to hosts of hostile virtualized environments. In *Proceedings of the CanSecWest applied security conference* (pp. 1–10).

Pearce, M., Zeadally, S., & Hunt, R. (2013). Virtualization: Issues, security threats, and solutions. *ACM Computing Surveys (CSUR), 45*(2), 17.

Raines, G. (2009). Cloud computing and SOA. Service Oriented architecture (SOA) series, systems engineering at MITRE. Retrieved March 23, 2015 from www.mitre.org.

Vmware. (2015). 5 *Essential characters of a winning virtualization platform*. Retrieved August, 2017 from https://www.vmware.com/content/.../pdf/solutions/vmw-5-essential-characteristics-ebook.pdf.

Chapter 4
Reliability Metrics Formulation

Abbreviations

CSP	Cloud Service Provider
CC	Cloud Consumer
API	Application Program Interface
CSCC	Cloud Standards Customer Council
RTO	Recovery Time Objective
RPO	Recovery Process Objective

Reliability of a product or service requires that it performs as per its specifications. The quality attributes are considered as reliability metrics because reliability is not only correcting errors but also observing correctness in the overall working. The intermediate quality of the process will also count for the overall reliability of the product or services. The quality attributes of various concepts like SOA, virtualization and quality standards described in Chap. 3 are quantified in this chapter using appropriate formula. This will help to achieve a single value between 0 and 1 for each metric. These values are then applied into the model proposed in Chap. 5 to evaluate reliability of cloud services. Attributes like availability, security, customer support, fault tolerance, interoperability, disaster recovery measures are common for all type of cloud services like IaaS, PaaS, and SaaS. Apart from this there are few more model specific attributes. For example, IaaS model specific quality attributes are load balancing, sustainability, elasticity, throughput, and efficiency. Specific quality attributes of SaaS model are functionality, customization facility, data migration, support, and monitoring. For PaaS model, binding and unbinding support for composable multi-tenant services and scaling of platform services are some of the specific attributes that are to be considered. This chapter lists reliability attributes for IaaS, PaaS, and SaaS service models along with its formulation.

V. Kumar and R. Vidhyalakshmi, *Reliability Aspect of Cloud Computing Environment*, https://doi.org/10.1007/978-981-13-3023-0_4

4.1 Introduction

Reliability is often considered as one of the quality factors. ISO 9126, an international standard for software evaluation has included reliability as one of the prime quality attribute along with functionality, efficiency, usability, portability, and maintainability. The CSMIC has identified various quality metrics to be used for comparison of cloud computing services (www.csmic.org). These are collectively named as SMI holding metrics which includes accountability, assurance, cost, performance, usability, privacy, and security. In the SMI metric collections, reliability is a mentioned sub factor of assurance metric, which deals with failure rate of service availability (Garg et al. 2013). IEEE 982.2-1988 states that a software reliability management program should encompass a balanced set of user-quality attributes along with identification of intermediate quality objective. The main requirement of high reliable software is the presence of high-quality attributes at each phase of development life cycle with the main intention of error prevention (Rosenberg et al. 1998). Mathematical assurance for the presence of high-quality attributes can further be used to evaluate the reliability of the entire product or services.

For example, consider a mobile phone. The reliability of mobile phone will be evaluated based on the number of failures that occur during a time period. The failures might occur due to mobile performance slow down, application crash, quick battery drain, Wi-Fi connectivity issues, poor call quality, random crashes, etc. The best way to assure failure resistant mobile phone is to include checks at each step of mobile phone manufacturing. If the steps were performed as per specifications following all standards and quality checks, then the failures will reduce to a greater extent. Reduced failures will increase the overall reliability of the product.

Metrics quantification is already explained in previous chapter. A quick recap of the metric categorization as given below

i. Expectation-based metrics (Type I) gathered from the business requirements of the user.
ii. Usage-based metrics (Type II) gathered from the existing users of the cloud products or service to check the performance assurance.
iii. Standard-based metrics (Type III).

Type II metric have further categorization based on the type of values that are accepted from the existing customers. If the gathered values are numeric and the match between assured and actual has to be calculated, then chi-square test method is used. If the value captured from the feedback is dichotomous having "yes" or "no" values, then binomial distribution method is used to calculate the reliability value of those metrics. Some of the assurance of the metric is provided as a simple statement in SLA without any numerical value. Performance values of these metrics are gathered as a count value from the users and are evaluated using simple division method. Further detailed information on quantification method is available in Sect. 3.5.

The reliability metric discussion in this chapter is divided as common metrics and model specific metrics. Under each model, IaaS, PaaS, and SaaS, metrics specific to model and the hierarchical framework of all the metrics is also provided. As discussed already these metrics are taken from various literature and standards documentation available. As the cloud computing paradigm is evolving rapidly, these metrics have to be updated time and again.

4.2 Common Cloud Reliability Metrics

Some of the reliability metrics are so vital that it will be present in all types of cloud service models. These are being considered as common cloud reliability metrics and are discussed below.

4.2.1 *Reliability Metrics Identification*

Common metrics irrespective of the service models are availability, support hours, scalability, usability, adherence to SLA, security certificates, built-in security, incidence reporting, regulatory compliance and disaster management.

i. *Availability*

This metric indicates the ability of cloud product or service that is accessible and usable by the authorized entity at the time of demand. This is one of the key Service Level Objective and is specified using numeric values in the SLA. The availability values such as 99.5, 99.9, or 99.99% that is mentioned in SLA will help to attract customers. Hence it is imperative to include it as one of the reliability metric to ensure continuity of service.

Availability is measured in terms of uptime of the service. The measurement should also include the planned downtime for maintenance. The period of calculation could be daily, monthly or yearly in terms of hours, minutes, or seconds. The uptime calculation using standard SLA formula is (Brussels 2014)

$$\text{Uptime} = T_{\text{avl}} - (T_{\text{tdt}} - T_{\text{mdt}}), \tag{4.1}$$

where

T_{avl} is the total agreed available time
T_{tdt} is the total downtime
T_{mdt} is the agreed maintenance downtime

All the fields should follow the same period and unit of measurement. If the downtime T_{tdt} is considered in hours per month then the rest of the values (T_{avl} and T_{mdt}) should be converted to hours per month. The assured available time is usually given as percentage in the SLA. It needs to be converted as hours per month. For example if the assured availability percentage is 99%, then the assured availability minutes per month is calculated as

Total hours per month = (30 * 24 = 720 h)
Availability percentage = 99%
Total uptime expected in hrs = 720 * 99/100 = 712.8 h/month
Total downtime would be = 720–712.80 = 7.2 h/month
Total down time of a year can be projected as 86.4/month
Allowed down time of a year is 3.6 days/year.

Likewise the downtime in terms of number of hours/month, hours/year or number of days/year can be calculated. 99% reliable systems have 3.65 days/year of down time, three nines (i.e.) 99.9% reliable systems have 0.365 days/year means 8.7 h/year of down time. For four nines 99.99% reliable systems have 52.56 min/year of down time and for five nines (i.e.) 99.999% reliable systems, the down time is 5.256 min/year of down time. Each addition of nine in cloud availability would increase the cost as assurance of increased availability is achieved with the help of enhanced backup. The other way out is to design a system architecture that handles the failovers during cloud outages. These can be implemented in any cloud technology with an extra design and configuration effort and should be tested rigorously. Failover solutions are generally less expensive to implement in the cloud due to on-demand or pay-as-you-go facility of cloud services.

ii. *Support*

This metric is used to measure the intensity of the support provided by the CSP to handle the issues and queries raised by the CCs. Maintaining strict quality of this metric is of utmost importance as positive feedback of this metric from existing customer will help to attracting more customers. The efficiency of support is measured in terms of the process and time by which the issues are resolved. Based on the specifications in the standard SLA guidelines the success probability of *support* is calculated with the help of three different factors (Brussels 2014).

Support hours → the value of this factor like 24 × 7 or 09–18 hrs indicates the assured working hours during which a CC can communicate with CSP for support or inquiry.
Support responsiveness → this factor indicates the maximum amount of time taken by the CSP to respond to CCs request or inquiry. This refers to the time within which the resolution process starts. It denotes only the start of the resolution process and is does not include completion of resolution.
Resolution time → the value of this factor specifies the target time taken to completely resolve CCs service requests. Example, assurance in the SLA that any reported problem will be resolved within 24 hrs of service request generation.

iii. *Scalability*

This metric is used to identify the efficiency with which dynamic provisioning feature of cloud is implemented. Scalability is an important feature which provides dynamic provisioning of applications, development platforms or IT resources to accommodate requirement spikes and surges. This also eliminates extra investments for seasonal requirements. The additional resources that are procured to satisfy the seasonal needs remain idle for most part of the year, thus reducing the optimum utilization of resources. Scaling can be done either by upgrading the existing resource capability or by adding additional resources. Horizontal scalability (scale-out) and vertical scalability (scale-up) are the two types of scaling. In horizontal scaling multiple hardware and software entities are connected as single unit for working. In vertical scaling, the capacities of existing resources are increased instead of adding new type of resources.

iv. *Usability*

Usability refers to the effectiveness, satisfaction, and efficiency with which specified users achieve specified goals in product usage or service utilization. Structure, consistency, navigation, searchability, feedback, control, and safety are the elements in which sites normally fail in efficiency (Marja and Matt 2002). ISO 9241 is a usability standard specification that started with basic human computer interaction using visual display terminal in 1980s. Now it has grown massively covering gamut of user experience features such as human centered design for interactive systems, software accessibility standards, standards for usability test reports, etc. The context of usability standards could be desktop computing, mobile computing, or ubiquitous computing. The usability of any cloud product or service relies on the user-centered design process (Stanton et al. 2014). Being an extension of existing computing environment, cloud is assumed to be readily usable. Standards related to usability and the desired usability features required for cloud products are listed below (www.usabilitynet.org)

a. Efficient, effective, and satisfactory use of the product or service
b. Capability to be used across different devices
c. Customizable user interface or interaction
d. Offline data access provision
e. Capability of organization to include user centered design

v. *Adherence to SLA*

Service Level Agreement (SLA) is a binding agreement between the provider and the customer of cloud product or services. It acts as a measuring scale to check the effective rendering of the services. Effective rendering refers to the service rendering as per assurance. It contains information that covers different jurisdiction due to the geographically distributed and global working nature of cloud services. Currently the SLA terminology varies from provider to provider and this increases the complexity in understanding SLA. This has been addressed by C-SIG-SLA, a group formed by the European commission in liaison with ISO Cloud Computing working group by devising standardization guidelines for cloud computing SLA (Brussels 2014). This is done with prime intention to bring clarity of the agreement terms and also to make it comprehensive and comparable.

The SLA contains Service Level Objectives (SLOs) specifying the assured efficiency level of the services provided by the CSP. Due to the different types of service provisioning and globally distributed list of customer the SLOs includes various specifications. The specifications required by the users have to be chosen depending on the business requirements. Various SLOs mentioned in the SLA are

a. Availability
b. Response time and throughput
c. Efficient simultaneous access to resources
d. Interoperability with on-premise applications
e. Customer support
f. Security incidence reporting
g. Logging and monitoring
h. Vulnerability management
i. Service charge specification
j. Data mirroring and backup facility

The above list needs to be updated based on the technology and business model developments.

vi. *Security Certificates*

The presence of this metric is essential to give assurance of security to the customers. Due to the integrated working model of cloud services, a set of certification acquisitions are important. A certified CSP stands high chance of being selected by the customers as it provides more confidence for the potential customer on the provider. The organizations such as ISACA, AICPA, CoBIT, and NIST have provided frameworks and certifications for evaluating IT security. Each certification has different importance. The Service Organization Control reports such as SOC1 and SOC2 contains details about the cloud organization working. SOC1 report contains the SSAE 16 audit details certifying the internal control design adequacy to meet the quality working requirement. SOC2 report formerly identified as SAS70 report which is specific for SaaS providers contain comprehensive report to certify availability, security, processing integrity, and confidentiality. The list of certificates that can be acquired with its validity is given in Table 4.1 (www.iso.org, www.infocloud.gov.hk).

vii. *Built-In Security*

Robust, verifiable, and flexible authentication and authorization is an essential built-in feature of a cloud product or service. This will help to enable secure data sharing among applications or storage locations. All the standard security built-in features expected to be present has been listed in Table 4.2. It is designed in accordance to the CSA, CSCC recommendations and industry suggestions. This list needs to be updated periodically based on CSA policy updations and cloud industry developments. The table also has two columns "Presence in SLA" and "Customer Input". These two columns are used for the reliability calculations of *built-in security* metric and are explained in the next section.

Table 4.1 List of security certifications

Certificate/Reports	Description	Validity
ISO/IEC 27001:2013	Information security management system requirements. It includes standards for outsourcing	3 years
ISO/IEC 27018:2014	Controls and guidelines for protection of personally identifiable information in public clouds	3 years
SOCI (SSAE 16) report	Reports on controls relevant to the users entities. Emphasizes on internal control over financial controls	Nil
SOC 2 Type I and II report	Reports on controls relevant to availability, confidentiality, security and processing integrity to provide assurance about the organization	Nil
ISO/IEC 27031	Provides guidance on the concepts and principles of ICT in ensuring business continuity	3 years
CSA STAR certificate	Assessment based on CCM v3.x and ISO/IEC 27001:2013	2 years
TRUSTe certificate	A leading privacy standards to provide strong privacy protection	
SysTrust report	Ensures the reliability of the system against availability, integrity and security	1 year

viii. *Incidence Reporting*

The unwanted or unexpected event or series of events that involves the intentional or accidental misuse of information is considered as information security incidence. Any breach of security will subsequently affect the business operations. Organizations are expected to have strong incident management system to detect, notify, evaluate, react, and learn from the security incidents. This is of prime importance in cloud scenario as the CSPs have to handle huge data from various customers. The CSPs should intimate the details about the security incidence and its rectification to CCs so as to plane risk mitigation measures. Once informed about the security breach the cloud customers can holdup the crucial business operations until the rectification is done. Reporting security incidences minimizes the impact on integrity, availability, and confidentiality of the cloud data and application. Successful incidence management should be in place for

a. Mitigating the impact of IT security incidences.
b. Identifying the root cause for the incidence to avoid future occurrence of the similar IT security incidences.
c. Capturing, protecting, and preserving all information with respect to security incident for forensic analysis.
d. Ensuring that all customers are aware of the incident.
e. Protecting the reputation of the company by following the above steps.

ix. *Regulatory Compliance*

Laws that protect data privacy and information security vary from country to country and compliance to the law is a complex task due to its distributed working method

Table 4.2 Built-in security features

S. No.	Built-in feature	Presence in SLA	Customer input
1	Controlled access points using physically secured perimeters		
2	Secure area authorization		
3	Fine grain access control		
4	Single sign-on feature		
5	Presence of double factor authentication		
6	Data asset catalog maintenance of all data stored in the cloud		
7	Encryption of data at rest and in motion		
8	Handling of both structured and unstructured data		
9	Data isolation in multi-tenant environment		
10	Data confidentiality (non-disclosure of confidential data to unauthorized users)		
11	Data integrity (authorized data modification)		
12	Network traffic screening		
13	Network IDS and IPS		
14	Data protection against loss or breach during exit process		
15	Automatic web vulnerability scans and penetration testing		
16	Integration of provider security log with enterprise security management system		
17	Power or critical service failure mitigation plans		
18	Incidence response plan in case of security breaches due to DDoS attacks		

(Tech Target 2015). Various compliance certificates and their detailed description are given in Table 4.3 (Singh and Kumar 2013).

x. *Disaster Management*

The operational disturbances need to be mitigated to ensure operational resiliency. Contingency plans which is also termed as Disaster Recovery (DR) plans are used to ensure business continuity. The aim of DR is to provide the organization with a way to recover data or implement various failover mechanisms in the event of man-made or natural disasters. The motive of DR plans is to ensure business continuity. Most DR plans include procedures for making availability of server, data, and storage through remote desktop access facility. These are maintained and manipulated by CSPs. There must be effective failover system to second site at times of hardware or software failure. Failback must also be in place which will ensure returning back to the original system if the failures are resolved. The organization on its part must ensure the availability of required network resources and bandwidth for transfer of data between primary data sites to cloud storage. The organization must also ensure

Table 4.3 Compliance certificate requirement

Compliance certificate	Description
US-EU Safe Harbor	This certificate is essential to establish global compliance standard and establish data protection measures that are required for cross-border data transfer. Possession of this certificate will ensure the European Union that the US organizations will conform to the EU regulations regarding the privacy protection
HIPAA	This deals with privacy of health information and is essential for health care applications. It has guidelines outlining the usage and disclosure of confidential health information
PCI DSS	This is essential for the products which may accept, store and process card holder data to perform card payments through Internet transactions. It has standard technical and operating procedures to safeguard the card holder's identity
FISMA	Federal Information Security Management Act provides security for the private data and also the penalization procedure in case of the violation of the act
GAPP	Generally Accepted Privacy Principles are laid out to protect the privacy of the individual data in business activities. The privacy principles are updated depending on the increasing complexity of businesses

proper encryption of the data which are leaving the organization. Testing of these DR activities must be carried out on isolated networks without affecting the operational data activity (Rouse 2016).

SLAs for cloud disaster recovery must include guaranteed uptime, Recovery Point Objective (RPO) and Recovery Time Objective (RTO). The service cost of cloud based DR will depend on the speed with which the failover is expected. Faster failover needs high cost investments.

xi. *Financial Metrics*

The final selection of the product needs to include financial metric consideration also. In order to identify the financial viability of the product, this metric is used as a deciding tool. The main objective is to assist the CCs in selecting the best cloud product or services based on their business requirement and also within planned budget. TCO reduction, low cost startup and increased ROI are the metrics related to financial benefits of cloud implementations.

TCO reduction is one of the prime entities in cloud adoption factors. The organizations need not do heavy initial investment which reduces TCO drastically.

Low startup cost is the reason for TCO reduction. Minimum infrastructure investment requirement for clouds usage is PC purchase and Internet connection setup.

The profitability of any investment is judged by its ROI. The ROI value gets better in a span of time. The procedure to calculate ROI of cloud applications is mentioned in formula 4.24.

4.2.2 Quantification Formula

The metrics identified in the previous section is quantified using the categories explained in Chap. 3. Depending on the user from whom the inputs are accepted and the type of value that is accepted from the users, metric quantification method is decided. Quantification formula for common metrics is given below.

i. *Availability (Type II Metric)*

The probability of success of this metric for a cloud product or service is calculated based on the exact monthly uptime hours gathered from existing customers. This is considered as the observed uptime value for availability. This is compared with the assured uptime mentioned on in the SLA using chi-square test. The corresponding success probability is calculated based on the chi-square value having the degree of freedom as number of customers-1. The period of data collection and the unit of measurement used for uptime must be the same.

The formula for calculating chi-square value is

$$\mathrm{CHI}_{\mathrm{AVL}} = \sum_{i=1}^{n} \frac{(\mathrm{avl}_{\mathrm{o}} - \mathrm{avl}_{\mathrm{e}})^2}{\mathrm{avl}_{\mathrm{e}}}, \tag{4.2}$$

where

$\mathrm{avl}_{\mathrm{o}}$ is the observed average uptime for 6 months
$\mathrm{avl}_{\mathrm{e}}$ is the assured uptime for 6 months
n is the total customers surveyed

Based on $\mathrm{CHI}_{\mathrm{AVL}}$ value and the degree of freedom as $(n - 1)$ the probability Q value is calculated. Q calculations can be done through websites available. One of the sites is (https://www.fourmilab.ch/rpkp/experiments/analysis/chiCalc.html). It is used in the browser that supports Javascript.

ii. *Support Hours (Type II Metric)*

The reliability of this metric is calculated based on three different values such as support hours, support response time, and resolution time. These values are already assured in the SLA which is taken as expected values. The actual performance of service or product is gathered from existing customers. Chi-square test is applied to check for the best fit. Formula to calculate support hours is

$$R_{\mathrm{shrs}} = \frac{\text{No. of successful calls placed during working hours}}{\text{Total no. of calls attempted during working hours}} \tag{4.3}$$

Along with support hours, support responsiveness, and resolution time factors need to be calculated as follows:

$$R_{\mathrm{resp}} = \frac{\text{No. of services responded within maximum time}}{\text{Total no. of services done}} \tag{4.4}$$

$$R_{\text{rt}} = \frac{\text{No. of services requests completed within target time}}{\text{Total no. of requests serviced}} \tag{4.5}$$

After calculation of these sub-factors final support hours evaluation is done based on the average of all three values R_{shrs}, R_{resp}, and R_{rt} and the formula for calculation is

$$R_{\text{Support}} = \frac{\frac{\sum_{i=1}^{n} R_{\text{shrs}}(i)}{n} + \frac{\sum_{i=1}^{n} R_{\text{resp}}(i)}{n} + \frac{\sum_{i=1}^{n} R_{\text{rt}}(i)}{n}}{3}, \tag{4.6}$$

where

n is the total number of customers involved in the feedback
$R_{\text{shrs}}(i)$ is the support hours reliability of the ith customer
$R_{\text{resp}}(i)$ is the support responsiveness reliability of the ith customer
$R_{\text{rt}}(i)$ is the resolution time reliability of the ith customer

iii. *Scalability (Type II Metric)*

The scalability metrics is measured as the time taken to scale. It is mentioned in the SLA as a range value ($S_{\max}$ and $S_{\min}$). $S_{\max}$ is the maximum time limit to scale and $S_{\min}$ is the minimum time limit to scale. The scaling process done within limits is considered as a success and the process that takes time beyond $S_{\max}$ is considered as failure. The metric is calculated based on the number of scaling done and umber of successful scaling process based on the feedback value input from existing customer. The formula used is

$$R_{\text{SCL}} = \frac{\sum_{i=1}^{m} \sum_{x=0}^{c_i} \binom{n}{x} p^x q^{n-x}}{m}, \tag{4.7}$$

where

m denotes the number of customers surveyed
c_i denotes the count of successful scaling done by ith customer
n denotes the total number of scaling done by ith customer
p denotes the probability of scaling to be success which is 0.5

iv. *Usability (Type I Factor)*

The measurement of this metric is based on the input accepted from the prospective and hence it is a type I metric. This factor is measured in terms of the presence of these usability features in the product. The more the count of the feature present the more will be the usability. It is calculated as

$$R_{\text{USBLTY}} = \frac{\text{No. of usability features present}}{\text{Total number of usability features}} \tag{4.8}$$

Total number of usability features in a cloud product or service has to be gathered from the standard specifications. These can be done by CCs or the reliability calculation model explained in next chapter has a cloud broker system which will assist customers in listing the usability features.

v. *Adherence to SLA (Type II Metric)*

This metric is calculated based on the usage value accepted from the existing users of the cloud product or services. Users have to provide the total number of items for which SLA adherence is required. The adherence to SLA metric is measured using the feedback from the existing cloud product customers. The measurement is done by comparing the assured objectives by the CSP with the experienced objective of the CC using Chi-square test. From the Chi-square value the success probability to keep up with the assured SLO is identified.

$$\mathrm{CHI}_{\mathrm{sla}} = \sum_{i=1}^{n} \frac{\left(\mathrm{SLO}_{\mathrm{req}} - \mathrm{SLO}_{\mathrm{act}}\right)^2}{\mathrm{SLO}_{\mathrm{req}}}, \tag{4.9}$$

where

$\mathrm{SLO}_{\mathrm{req}}$ is the number of objectives required to be maintained
$\mathrm{SLO}_{\mathrm{act}}$ is the number of objectives actually maintained
n is the total customers from whom the feedback is gathered

Based on $\mathrm{CHI}_{\mathrm{SLA}}$ value and the degree of freedom as $(n - 1)$ the probability Q value is calculated. Q calculations can be done through websites available. One of the sites is (https://www.fourmilab.ch/rpkp/experiments/analysis/chiCalc.html). It is used in the browser that supports Javascript. This will be the R_{sla} value.

vi. *Security Certificates (Type I Metric)*

This is a type I metric which is calculated based on the input from the prospective users of cloud services. The inputs are provided based on the business requirements. Periodic auditing which is an evaluation process has to be carried out to identify the degree to which the audit criteria are fulfilled. This auditing is performed by third party or external organization. This enables systematic and documented process for providing evidence of the standard conformance maintained by CSP. The conformance to standards and security certificates also increases the trust of the CC on the services provided. All certificates needs to be renewed and should be within expiry date limits. The required security certificate details are accepted from the CC and the possession of the valid required security certificate is used to measure this factor.

$$R_{\text{sec-cert}} = \frac{\text{Count of possession of required valid security certificates}}{\text{Total count of the required valid security certificates}} \tag{4.10}$$

vii. *Built-In Security (Type II and Type III Metric)*

This metric is calculated as the combination of Type II and type III metric calculations. The "Presence in *SLA*" and "Customer Input" column of Table 4.1 has to be filled. The "Presence in *SLA*" column is filled with the product security specification given in the *SLA*. The "Customer Input" column holds the feedback value gathered from customer based on their experience of security issues or satisfaction. The formulas used for the *built-in security* metric calculation are

$$R_{\text{SF}} = R_{\text{fg}} - (1 - R_{\text{fa}}), \tag{4.11}$$

where R_{fg} is reliability of the guaranteed security features and is calculated based on the features mentioned in the brochure against the features mentioned in the standards. Type III metric calculation is used here. The formula for calculation is

$$R_{\text{fg}} = \frac{\text{Number of security features guaranteed in SLA}}{\text{Total number of desired built-in security features}} \tag{4.12}$$

R_{fa} is the reliability of the provider to adhere to the security features guaranteed and is calculated using chi-square method (type II metric method) to find the best fit of the assured value with the actual value

$$R_{\text{fa}} = \sum_{i=1}^{n} \frac{(F_{\text{o}} - F_{\text{e}})^2}{F_{\text{e}}}, \tag{4.13}$$

where

n is the total number of customers being surveyed
F_{o} is the observed count of features rendered
F_{e} is the expected count of assured feature based on SLA

viii. *Incidence Reporting (Type II Factor)*

Security incidences are expected to be low but if it happens it has to be reported to the customer. Based on the reporting efficiency the value of this metric is calculated. The efficiency can be gathered from the existing customers. The formula to calculate the reliability of incidence reporting metric is

$$R_{\text{sec-inc-rep}} = \frac{\sum_{i=1}^{n} \text{REP}_{\text{ef}}(i)}{n}, \tag{4.14}$$

where

n is the number of customer involved in feedback
REP_{ef} is the reporting efficiency experienced by the customer and is calculated using the formula

$$\text{REP}_{\text{ef}} = \frac{\text{No. of incidences reported}}{\text{Total number of incidences}} \tag{4.15}$$

The total number of incidences that occurred can be gathered from the dash board of the cloud product or services.

ix. *Regulatory Compliance (Type I Metric)*

This metric is calculated based on the input provided by the customers who are willing to adopt cloud product or services. Based on their business requirements, the compliance certificate requirements have to be laid out. This is checked against the presence of the required certificates with the provider.

Mere certificate possession does not guarantee the conformance to compliance. A valid certificate possession is required. This is achieved by timely renewal of essential certificates. The required compliance certificate details are accepted from the CC and the possession of the valid required compliance certificate details are gathered from the dashboard or from the brochure of the product or service. These two values are used to calculate the reliability of *regulatory compliance* metric.

$$R_{\text{comp-cert}} = \frac{\text{Possession of required valid compliance cert. count}}{\text{Total count of the required compliance certificates}} \tag{4.16}$$

x. *Disaster Management (Type I Metric)*

This metric is calculated based on the input that are accepted from the current users of cloud product or services. The DR capabilities are inherent part of the cloud service where the data replication takes place. This metric is very important for Small and Medium Enterprise (SME) customers as they do not possess in-house IT skills to take care of risk mitigation measures. The role of CCs is to ensure the suitability of the DR plans with their business requirements. The organizations opting for cloud DR should have contingency plans apart from the cloud DR investment. This is needed to ensure business continuity in worst case scenario. The DR plan of the CSP should specify comprehensive list of DR features guaranteed to be maintained by them. The reliability of this factor is calculated as

$$R_{\text{DR}} = \frac{\text{Count of required DR features offered by CSP}}{\text{Total number of required DR features}} \tag{4.17}$$

xi. *Financial Metrics*

TCO metric comparison of the existing on-premise application with that of the cloud offering will give the TCO reduction efficiency. The percentage of TCO reduction is calculated as

$$\text{TCO}_{\text{reduce}} = \frac{\text{TCO}_{\text{on-premise}} - \text{TCO}_{\text{cloud}}}{\text{TCO}_{\text{on-premise}}} \tag{4.18}$$

The TCO calculation is done based on the summation of initial investment referred to as upfront cost, operational cost, and annual disinvestment costs (Kumar Vidhyalakshmi 2013). Upfront cost is a one-time cost and other two costs are calculated from the second year.

$$\mathrm{TCO} = C_{\mathrm{u}} + \sum_{i=2}^{n} (C_{\mathrm{ad}} + C_{\mathrm{o}}), \tag{4.19}$$

where

C_{u} is the upfront cost and is calculated as

$$C_{\mathrm{u}} = C_{\mathrm{h}} + C_{\mathrm{d}} + C_{\mathrm{t}} + C_{\mathrm{ps}} + C_{\mathrm{cust}}, \tag{4.20}$$

where

C_{h} denotes the cost of hardware
C_{d} denotes the cost of software development
C_{t} denotes the staff training cost for proper utilization of software
C_{ps} is the professional consultancy cost
C_{cust} is the customization cost to suit the business requirement
C_{ad} is the annual disinvestment cost and is calculated as

$$C_{\mathrm{ad}} = C_{\mathrm{hmaint}} + C_{\mathrm{smaint}} + C_{\mathrm{pspt}} + C_{\mathrm{cust}}, \tag{4.21}$$

where

C_{hmaint} denotes the hardware maintenance cost
C_{smaint} denotes the software maintenance cost
C_{pspt} denotes the professional support cost
C_{cust} is the customization cost to incorporate business changes
C_{o} is the operational cost and is calculated as

$$C_{\mathrm{o}} = C_{\mathrm{inet}} + C_{\mathrm{pow}} + C_{\mathrm{infra}} + C_{\mathrm{adm}}, \tag{4.22}$$

where

C_{inet} refers to the Internet cost
C_{pow} refers to the cost of power utilized for ICT operations
C_{infra} refers to the floor space infrastructure cost
C_{adm} refers to the administration cost

The increase in ROI is calculated based on the comparison of on-premise ROI with the ROI after cloud adoption.

$$\mathrm{ROI}_{\text{increase}} = \frac{\mathrm{ROI}_{\text{on-premise}} - \mathrm{ROI}_{\text{SaaS}}}{\mathrm{ROI}_{\text{on-premise}}} \tag{4.23}$$

ROI of any business activity is calculation as (Vidhyalakshmi and Kumar 2016)

$$\mathrm{ROI} = \frac{\text{Gain from investment} - \text{Cost of investment}}{\text{Cost of investment}} \tag{4.24}$$

4.3 Infrastructure as a Service

Basic IT resources such as server for processing, storage of data and communication network are offered as services in Infrastructure as a Service (IaaS) model. Virtualization is the base technique being followed in IaaS for efficient resource sharing along with low cost and increased flexibility (CSCC 2015). Management of resources lies with the service provider where as some of the backup facility may be left with the customers. Usage of IaaS is like conversion of the data center activity of the organization to cloud environment. IaaS is more under the control of operators who deals with the decision of server allocation, storage capacity and network topologies to be used.

4.3.1 Reliability Metrics Identification

Some of the metrics that are of specific importance to IaaS operations are location awareness, notification reports, sustainability, adaptability, elasticity throughput.

i. *Location Awareness*

Data location refers to the geographic location of CCs data storage or data processing location. The fundamental design principle of cloud application permit data to be stored, processed, and transferred to any data center, server or devices operated by the service provider that are geographically distributed. This is basically done to provide service continuity in case of any data center service disruption or to share the over workload of one data center with another less loaded data center to increase the resource utilization. Choosing a correct data center is a crucial task as it will be complex and time consuming to relocate hardware. Wrong choice will also lead to loss due to bad investment. A list of tips to be followed before choosing data center and also to avoid bad decision is given below (Zeifman 2015).

a. Explore the physical location of the data center if possible
b. Connectivity evaluation
c. Security standards understanding
d. Understanding bandwidth limit and bursts costs
e. Power management and energy backup plans at data centers

Data or processing capacity might also be transferred to the locations, where the legislation does not guarantee the required level of data protection. The lawfulness of the cross-border data transfers should be associated with any one of the appropriate measures viz. safe harbor arrangements, binding corporate rules or EU model clauses (Brussels 2014).

Table 4.4 Data center energy consumption contribution

Component	Energy consumption (%)
IT equipments	30
Cooling devices	42
Electrical equipments	28

ii. *Notification Reports*

CSPs have more responsibilities for cloud resource maintenance and are expected to retain the trust of CCs. Updation of terms of service, service charge change notifications, payment date reminders, privacy policy modifications, new service release information, planned or unplanned maintenance period notices and service upgrade details need to be notified to the customers. The CCs on their part need to register and update contact information with the CSP. Some CSPs offer option to choose the communication preferences.

iii. *Sustainability*

Four main components of data center are network devices, cooling devices, storage server and electrical devices. A typical data center has local area network and routers for connectivity, servers holding virtual machines and storage for processing, cooling devices and electrical devices. The energy overhead includes consumption by IT systems, cooling systems, power delivery components such as batteries, UPS, switch gears and generators (GeSI 2013). The percentage of energy consumption of the components used in the data centers is listed in Table 4.4.

The energy efficiency of the data center can be enhanced by achieving the maximum efficient utilization of non-IT equipment. The energy consumed by the data center is measured using the metric PUE (Power Usage Effectiveness) and DCiE (Data Center infrastructure Efficiency).

iv. *Adaptability*

Adaptability refers to the ability of the service provider to make changes in services based on the technology or customer requirements. This process needs to be completed without any disturbance to the existing infrastructure usage.

v. *Throughput*

Throughput is the metric that is used to evaluate the performance of the infrastructure. It depends on the parameters that affect the execution of the tasks such as infrastructure startup time, inter application communication time, data transfer time, etc. The throughput metric is different from service response time which refers to the time within which issues of the services are resolved. Detailed discussion about service and support is mentioned in Sect. 4.2.1.

4.3.2 Quantification Formula

All IaaS specific metrics are quantified using metrics categories explained in Sect. 3.5.

i. *Location Awareness (Type II Metric)*

The CSPs are expected to notify the data movement details to the CCs to keep them aware of the data location and also to maintain openness and transparency of the operations. The CSPs provide the prospective geographic location list where the data could be moved and some of the providers also give option to choose the geographic location to store data. The efficiency of the location awareness is calculated based on the existing feedback from existing users. In SLA, assurance will be provided that they will stick to the chosen location. Compliance to this assurance is examined by enquiring users about reality. The count of correct data movements is captured from the existing users. If the data movement is to a location chosen by the user, then it is counted as correct data movement. The formula used for calculation is

$$R_{\mathrm{LA}} = \frac{\sum_{i=1}^{n} \mathrm{LA}_{\mathrm{eff}}(i)}{n}, \tag{4.25}$$

where

n is the number of customers considered for feedback
$\mathrm{LA}_{\mathrm{eff}}$ is the efficiency of data movement which is calculated as

$$\mathrm{LA}_{\mathrm{eff}} = \frac{\text{Number data movement to the listed locations}}{\text{Total number of data movements}} \tag{4.26}$$

ii. *Notification Reports (Type II Metric)*

Evaluation of this metric is done based on the feedback accepted from the existing users. Transparency assurance in SLA will be achieved through notifications to the customers. This includes distribution of details with respect to any policy changes, payment charge changes, downtime issues, security breaches to the customers.

Efficiency of notification is measured as

$$\mathrm{EFF}_{\mathrm{notify}} = \frac{\text{Number of notification of changes}}{\text{Total number of changes}} \tag{4.27}$$

The reliability of this factor is calculated as the average of the notification efficiency feedback from existing customers.

$$R_{\text{notify}} = \frac{\sum_{i=1}^{n} \text{EFF}_{\text{notify}}(i)}{n}, \tag{4.28}$$

where

n	denotes the number of customers surveyed
$\text{EFF}_{\text{notify}}(i)$	denotes the notification efficiency of the ith customer

iii. *Sustainability*

DCiE is the percentage of the total facility power that is utilized by the IT equipment such as compute, storage, and network. PUE is calculated as the ratio of the total energy utilized by the data center to the energy utilized by the IT equipment. The ideal PUE value of the data center is 1.0. The formula for calculating PUE which is the inverse of DCiE is (Garg et al. 2013)

$$\text{PUE} = \frac{\text{Total Facility Energy}}{\text{IT Equipment Energy (DCiE)}} \tag{4.29}$$

The Data center Performance per Energy (DPPE) is another metric that is used to correlate the performance of the datacenter with the emission from the data center. The formula for calculating DPPE is (Garg et al. 2013)

$$\text{DPPE} = \text{ITEU} \times \text{ITEE} \times \frac{1}{\text{PUE}} \times \frac{1}{1 - \text{GEC}}, \tag{4.30}$$

where ITEU is IT Equipment Utilization which is the average utilization factor of all IT equipments of the data center. It denotes the degree of energy saving accomplished using virtualization and optimal utilization of IT resources. It is calculated as

$$\text{ITEU} = \frac{\text{Total actual energy consumed by IT devices}}{\text{Total specification of energy by manufacturer}} \tag{4.31}$$

ITEE is IT Equipment Energy Efficiency that represents the energy saving of the IT devices due to efficient usage by extracting high processing capacity for single unit of power consumption. It is calculated as

$$\text{ITEE} = \frac{a \sum \text{Server capacity} + b \sum \text{Network capacity} + c \sum \text{Storage capacity}}{\text{Total energy specification provided by manufacturer}} \tag{4.32}$$

The parameters *a*, *b,* and *c* the weight co-efficient.

GEC represents the utilization of Renewable energy into the data center. It is calculated as

$$\text{GEC} = \frac{\text{Amount of Green Energy utilized}}{\text{Total DC power consumption}} \tag{4.33}$$

iv. *Adaptability (Type II Metric)*

This metric is measured using the time taken by the provider to adapt to the change. This is a type II metric as the efficiency of adaptability is accepted from the existing users. Any adaptability process that happens within the specific time delay is considered as successful adaptation and the one that goes beyond the allowed delay time is considered as failed adaptability. The formula to calculate this metric is

$$R_{\text{adapt}} = \frac{\sum_{i=1}^{n} \text{EFF}_{\text{adapt}}(i)}{n}, \tag{4.34}$$

where

n is the number of customers
$\text{EFF}_{\text{adapt}}$ is calculated as

$$\text{EFF}_{\text{adapt}} = \frac{\text{Number of successful adaptation process}}{\text{Total number of adaptation process}} \tag{4.35}$$

v. *Throughput*

It is the number of tasks that are completed by the cloud infrastructure in one unit of time. Assume an application has n tasks and are submitted to m number of machines at the cloud provider's end. Let $T_{m,n}$ be the total execution time of all the tasks. Let T_{o} be the time taken for the overhead processes. The formula to calculate throughput efficiency is (Garg et al. 2013)

$$R_{\text{Tput}} = \frac{n}{T_{m,n} + T_{\text{o}}} \tag{4.36}$$

4.4 Platform as a Service

Platform as a Service (PaaS) specifically targeted on application developers, provides an on-demand platform for development, deploy, and operated applications. PaaS includes diverse software platform and monitoring facilities. Software platform facilities include application development platform, analytics platform, integration platform, mobile back-end services, event-screening services, etc. Monitoring facilities include management, control, and deployment-related capabilities (CSCC 2017). CSP of PaaS deployment will take the responsibility of installation, operation and configuration of applications leaving besides the application coding to the cloud customer. PaaS offerings can also be expanded on the platform capability of middleware by providing diverse and growing set of APIs and services to application developers.

PaaS adoption also provides facilities that enable applications to take advantage of the native characteristics of cloud system without addition of any special code. This also facilitates building of "born on the cloud" applications without requirement of any specialized programming skills (CSCC 2015).

4.4.1 Reliability Metrics Identification

Metrics that specific to PaaS service models are audit logs, Tools for development, provision of runtime applications, portability, service provisioning, rapid deployment mechanism etc.

i. Audit Logs

Logs can be termed as "flight data recorder" of IT operations. Logging is the process of recording data related to the processes handled by servers, networking nodes, applications, client devices, and cloud service usages. The logging and monitoring activities are done by the CSP for cloud service. These log files are huge and the analyzing process is very complex. Centralized data logging needs to be followed by the CSP to reduce the complexity. Cloud based log management solutions are available that can be used to gain insight from the log entries and are identified as Logging as a Service. This is very essential in development environment as these log files are used for tracing errors and server process related activities.

The CC can use log files to monitor day-to-day cloud service usage details. These are also used by CCs for analyzing security breaches or failures if any. The parameters that will be captured in the log file, the accessibility of the log file by the CCs and the retention period of the log files will be mentioned in the SLA.

ii. *Development Tools*

PaaS service models aims to develop applications on the go. It also aims to streamline the development processes. It helps to support DevOps by removing the separation between development and operations. This separation is most common in in-house application development process. PaaS systems provide tools for code editors, code repositories, development, runtime code building, testing, security checking, and service provisioning. Tools also exist for control and analytics activities like monitoring, analytics services, logging facility, log analysis, analytics of app usage and dashboard visualization, etc.

iii. Portability

Many PaaS systems are designed for green field applications development where the applications are primarily designed to be built and deployed using cloud environment. These applications can be ported to any PaaS deployment with less or no modification. Sometimes there may be non-cloud based development framework applications that are hosted on to PaaS environment. This brings in some doubts like will the ported applications function without any errors or can it get the complete benefits of PaaS environment? (CSCC 2015).

4.4.2 Quantification Formula

The quantification of the PaaS specific metrics is as follows.

i. *Audit Logs (Type II Metric)*

This is type II metric as the efficiency of the logging process is gathered from the existing customers. Customer feedback is carried out to check the success or failure of log file accessibility and log data retention. The formula to calculate the reliability of the logging factor is

$$R_{\log} = \frac{\text{EFF}_{\text{log\_acc}} + \text{EFF}_{\text{log\_ret}}}{2}, \tag{4.37}$$

where

$\text{EFF}_{\text{log\_acc}}$ is the efficiency of the log data accessibility which is calculated using the cumulative distribution of the binomial function

$$\text{EFF}_{\text{log\_acc}} = \sum_{x=0}^{c} \binom{n}{x} p^x (1-p)^{n-x}, \tag{4.38}$$

where

n denotes the total number of customer surveyed.
c denotes the count of successful log file accessed
p denotes the probability of access to be success which is 0.5
$\text{EFF}_{\text{log\_ret}}$ is the efficiency of the log data retention which is calculated using the cumulative distribution of the binomial function

$$\text{EFF}_{\text{log\_ret}} = \sum_{x=0}^{c} \binom{n}{x} p^x (1-p)^{n-x}, \tag{4.39}$$

where

n denotes the total number of customer surveyed.
c denotes the count of successful log file retention
p denotes the probability of retention to be success which is 0.5

ii. *Development Tools (Type I Metric)*

This metric is used to evaluate the efficiency of the PaaS service provider in providing development environment. The presence of various development tools essential for rapid application development will increase the chances of selection. This is a type I metric as the evaluation is done based on the requirement of the PaaS developer. The formula for development tools reliability evaluation is

$$R_{\text{dev\_tool}} = \frac{\text{Tool}_i}{n}, \tag{4.40}$$

where

n is the total number of tools required by the developer
Tool_i is the development tools available with the PaaS provider

The final evaluated value of this metric is expected to be 1 indicating the presence of all the required tools.

iii. *Portability (Type III Metric)*

The efficiency of this metric is identified using the feedback from the existing customers. This metric is measured based on the efficiency of the portability process. Any portability process that ends in application execution without any errors or conversion requirement is considered as successful porting. If porting process takes more than the assured time or the ported process execution fails then it is considered as a failed porting process. As the measuring values are dichotomous with "success" and "failure", binomial method of type II metric calculation is used for portability metric evaluation.

$$R_{\text{port}} = \frac{\sum_{i=1}^{m} \sum_{x=0}^{c_i} \binom{n}{x} p^x q^{n-x}}{m}, \tag{4.41}$$

where

m denotes the number of developer surveyed
c_i denotes the count of successful porting done by ith developer
N denotes the total number of porting done by ith developer
p denotes the probability of successful porting which is 0.5

4.5 Software as a Service

Software as a Service (SaaS) is provisioning of complete application or application suite by CSP. It is expected that the application should cover the whole gamut of business process starting from simple mailing extending to ERP or e-business implementation. SaaS applications are developed as modules used by medium or small organization. Enterprise applications are also covered as SaaS offering, example CRM application of salesforce.com. The responsibility of development, deployment, maintenance of software and the hardware stack lies with CSP. This type of cloud models are often used by end-users. SaaS offerings can also be used with specialized front-end applications for enhanced usability. SaaS applications are mostly built using PaaS platform which has IaaS as its base for IT resources. This is referred to as cloud computing stack (CSCC 2015).

4.5.1 Reliability Metrics Identification

Apart from the metrics defined under Sect. 4.2 which are metrics common to all service models, there are few metrics that are specific to SaaS operations. SaaS applications are adopted mostly by MSME customers due to less IT overhead, faster time to market and controlling of entire application by CSPs. Entire business operation will depend on the failure free working SaaS and the various SaaS specific metrics are discussed below.

i. *Workflow Match*

Cloud product market is flooded with numerous applications to perform same business process. For example, SaaS products available for accounting processes are—FreshBooks, Quickbooks, Intact, Kashoo, Zoho Books, Clear Books, Wave Accounting, Financial Force, etc. Customers are faced with the herculean task of choosing a suitable product from a wide array of SaaS products. This metric can be used as a first filter to identify the product or products that are suitable for the business process. Not all organizations have same business processes and not all applications have same functionality. Some organizations have organized working while some have unorganized working. Some may want to stick to their operational profile and would want the software to be customized. Some may want the business streamlining and would want to include standard procedures in business so as to achieve global presence. This metric will provide an opportunity to analyze the business processes and list out the requirements.

ii. *Interoperability*

This refers to the ability of exchanging and mutual usage of information between two or more applications. These applications could be an existing on-premise application or the applications used from other CSPs. This is an essential feature of a SaaS product as they are built by integrating loosely coupled modules which needs proper orchestration so as to operate accurately and securely irrespective of platforms used or hosting locations. Some organizations may also have proprietary modules which need to be maintained along with cloud applications. In such cases the selected cloud applications has to interoperate with on-premise applications without any data loss and with less coding requirements. This success of this feature also assures the ability of the product to interact with other products offered by the same provider or by other providers. Maintaining high interoperability index also eliminates the risk of being locked in with a single provider.

Reliability of this metric is of major importance for those SaaS applications which are used along with the on-premise application execution. It also important in those cases in which, an organization uses SaaS products from various vendors to accomplish their tasks. The success of interoperability depends on the degree to which the provider uses open or published file formats, architecture, and protocols.

iii. *Ease of Migration*

Migration refers to the shifting of on-premise application to cloud based or migrating applications from one vendor to another. In any case, strategic planning is essential for migration in order to maintain business continuity during the migration process. Various costs factors such as subscription cost, network cost, upfront costs involved in migration needs to be analyzed using cost benefit analysis to justify the SaaS implementation. This process is not required and is not considered for green field applications, where cloud is used from the scratch for IT business implementation. This is mostly used by startups. SaaS implementation is assured to be a quick process but still needs a clear timeline specification for the actual implementation. Depending on the size of data that needs to be transferred, the migration strategies are planned. If the data runs to tera or peta bytes then the physical migration of data needs to be done to save the data transfer cost and huge time taken for the data transfer during which the business continuity will be affected. If the SaaS usage is by SME where data volume will be in giga bytes then data can be transferred through network. The main tasks that are identified to be carried out for migration are

a. Data conversion
b. Data transfer
c. Training for the staff to handle SaaS

A Work Breakdown Structure (WBS) can be created with clearly defined time limit for the tasks to be finished. The measurement of this factor is based on the time taken for the tasks mentioned. Data transfer time is not be included in the formulation as the transfer time is calculated based on the volume of data transfer rate per second. As this depends on the network traffic and transfer capacity at the customer end, this is not taken into consideration for vendor evaluation but is needed for migration process tracking. The deviation of the actual time taken from the time mentioned in WBS is used in migration value calculation.

iv. *Updation Frequency*

Customers prefer SaaS products to reduce IT overhead such as software maintenance, renewals, and upgradations. Good Software should be up-to-date to keep pace with the latest technology development which will eventually give competitive advantage. This is an essential feature for reliable SaaS product evaluation as this feature eliminates the technology overhead from the customer end and also reduces the cost and time invested to perform software upgradation process. The updations could be done for new feature inclusion or error fixes or new technology adaptation. The updation process should not affect the business continuity of existing customers. The feature updations of SaaS products will be effective if it is done based on the global customer feedback. Automatic updations and provisioning of the latest version eliminates the version compatibility issues.

v. *Backup Frequency*

The CSPs provide convenient and cost-effective automatic periodic backup and synchronization of data to offsite locations for the SaaS services. Three different types of backup sites exist such as hot site, warm site, and cold site. Hot sites are used for backup of critical business data as they are up and running continuously and the failover takes place within minimum lag time. These hot sites must be online and should be located away from the original site. Warm sites have the cost attraction than hot sites and are used for less critical operation backups. The failover process from warm sites takes more time than hot sites. The cold sites are the cheapest for backup operations but the switch over process is very time consuming when compared to hot and warm sites (www.Omnisecu.com). In addition to automatic backup processes, the CCs can utilize the data export facility to export data to another location or to another CSP to maintain continuity in case of disaster or failure.

Periodic backups are conducted automatically by CSP and had to be tested by CCs at specific interval of time. Local backups are expected to be completed within 24 h and offsite backups are taken daily or weekly based on the SaaS offering and business requirement. The choice of backup method option needs to be taken from the CCs.

vi. *Recovery Process*

Cloud recovery process such as automatic failover and redirection of users to replicated servers needs to be handled by CSP efficiently which enable the CCs to perform their operations even in times of critical server failure (BizTechReports 2010). The guaranteed *RPO* and *RTO* will be specified in the SLA. *RPO* indicates the acceptable time window between the recovery points. A smaller time window initiates the mirroring process of both persistent and transient data while a larger window will result in periodic backup process. *RTO* is the maximum amount of business interruption time (Brussels 2014). The CCs should prepare the recovery plans by determining the acceptable *RPO* and RTO for the services they use and ensure its adherence with the recovery plans of the CSP.

4.5.2 Quantification Formula

Quantification of metrics such a workflow match, interoperability, ease of migration, updation frequency, and recovery process are given importance in SaaS reliability evaluation.

i. *Workflow Match (Type I Metrics)*

This is a type I metric as the input for the metric is accepted from the customers who are willing to adopt a SaaS product for their business process. The metric measurement is accomplished by listing out the workflow requirements of the organizations as $R_1, R_2, R_3, \ldots, R_n$. The SaaS product that matches with all the requirements or with the maximum number of requirement is considered for further reliability calculation. The maximum number of requirements that needs to be met is set as $\mathrm{Req}_{\max}$. Organizations have to set the $\mathrm{Req}_{\max}$ value which can also be termed as threshold value. A vector has to be formed with values "1"s and "0"s. The requirements that are satisfied by the product are marked as 1 and not that are not satisfied is marked as 0. The count of the "1"s will give the workflow match value of the product. The formula to calculate the workflow match of a product is

$$R_{\mathrm{WFM}} = \frac{\sum_{i=1}^{n} \mathrm{Req}_i}{n}, \tag{4.42}$$

where

n is the total number of work flow requirements of the customer
Req_i is the matching work flow requirements of the product

The desired WFM metric value for a product is 1 which indicates that all the requirements are satisfied and the product is reliable in terms of work flow match.

ii. *Interoperability (Type I Metric)*

This metric is measured based on the facility to effortlessly transfer the data without loss of data or data being re-entered. Value for this metric is gathered from the prospective customers who are willing to adopt SaaS for their business operations; hence it is Type I metric. Greater efficiency of this metric can be achieved, if the data that are needed for interaction are in open standard file format (e.g. CSV file format, NoSQL format) so that it can be used without any conversion.

This factor is measured based on the time taken for the conversion process. Let $T_{\min}$, be the minimum allowed time for the conversion that is set by the customer. All the interacting modules that take more than $T_{\min}$ will eventually affect the interoperability of the product and is calculated as

$$R_{\mathrm{INTROP}} = \frac{\sum_{i=1}^{m} M_i}{n}, \tag{4.43}$$

where

M_i is the module whose data conversion time is $>T_{\min}$
n is the total number of modules that needs to interact

The desired value of INTROP is 1, an indication for the smooth interaction between modules with little or no conversion.

iii. *Ease of Migration (Type II Metric)*

This metric evaluation is done based on the data gathered from the existing customers who have used the SaaS product. Chi-square test is used to find the goodness of fit of the observed value with the expected value and its corresponding probability is calculated for both data conversion and training and their average is taken as the final migration value of the product.

$$R_{\mathrm{MIGR}} = \frac{R_{\mathrm{dc}} + R_{\mathrm{tr}}}{2}, \tag{4.44}$$

where

R_{dc} is the reliability of data conversion calculated from $MIGR_{dc}$
R_{tr} is the reliability of training for staff from $MIGR_{tr}$

$$R_{dc} = \sum_{i=1}^{n} \frac{(DC_o - DC_e)^2}{DC_e}, \tag{4.45}$$

where

DC_o is the actual data conversion time
DC_e is the assured or expected data conversion time
n is the total customers surveyed

$$R_{tr} = \sum_{i=1}^{n} \frac{(TR_o - TR_e)^2}{TR_e}, \tag{4.46}$$

where

TR_o is the actual time taken for training
TR_e is the assured or expected time for training
n is the total customers surveyed

iv. *Updation Frequency (Type II Metric)*

This metric measurement gives guarantee to the customers that they are in pace with the latest technology. The desired software updation frequency is 3–6 months and the assured frequency is specified in the SLA. The measurement of this factor is done based on the feedback accepted from existing customer feedback. The updation frequency is considered for a period of 24 months. The factor is calculated as

$$R_{UPFRQ} = \frac{\sum_{i=1}^{n} U_{ai}/n}{U_p}, \tag{4.47}$$

where

U_{ai} is the actual number of software updations experienced by customer i
n is the number of customers surveyed
U_p refers to the proposed number updations calculated based on the frequency updation specification of SLA with respect to the feedback period

v. *Backup Frequency (Type II Metric)*

The reliability of the backup frequency metric is calculated based on the feedback from the existing customers. The average of the cumulative efficiency of mirroring latency, data backup frequency and backup retention time will provide the reliability of this metric. These values are gathered for the duration of 6 months.

$$R_{\text{Backup}} = \frac{\frac{\sum_{i=1}^{n} R_{\text{mirror}}(i)}{n} + \frac{\sum_{i=1}^{n} R_{\text{bck-frq}}(i)}{n} + \frac{\sum_{i=1}^{n} R_{\text{brt}}(i)}{n}}{3}, \tag{4.48}$$

where

n is the total number of customers involved in the feedback

$R_{\text{mirror}}(i)$ is the mirroring reliability of the ith customer calculated using chi-square test of the assured latency and experienced latency

$$R_{\text{mirror}} = \sum_{i=1}^{n} \frac{(\text{ml}_o - \text{ml}_e)^2}{\text{ml}_e}, \tag{4.49}$$

where

ml_o is the observed mirror latency, ml_e is the assured mirror latency and n is the total customers surveyed

$R_{\text{bck-frq}}(i)$ is the data backup frequency reliability of the ith customer calculated using chi-square test of the assured frequency and experienced frequency

$$R_{\text{bck\_frq}} = \sum_{i=1}^{n} \frac{(\text{bf}_o - \text{bf}_e)^2}{\text{bf}_e}, \tag{4.50}$$

where

bf_o is the observed backup frequency, bf_e is the assured backup frequency and n is the total customers surveyed

$R_{\text{brt}}(i)$ is the backup retention time reliability of the ith customer calculated using chi-square test of the assured retention time and experienced retention time

$$R_{\text{brt}} = \sum_{i=1}^{n} \frac{(\text{brt}_o - \text{brt}_e)^2}{\text{brt}_e}, \tag{4.51}$$

where

brt_o is the observed backup retention time

brt_e is the assured backup retention time and n is the total customers surveyed

vi. *Recovery Process (Type II Metric)*

The reliability of the recovery process is based on the successful recovery which is completed within RTO and without any errors. The recovery processes not within *RTO* or within *RTO* and with errors are identified as failure with respect to the reliability calculations. This metric is based on the input from existing customers. The recovery process metric for a product is calculated as the average of successful recoveries of the existing customers.

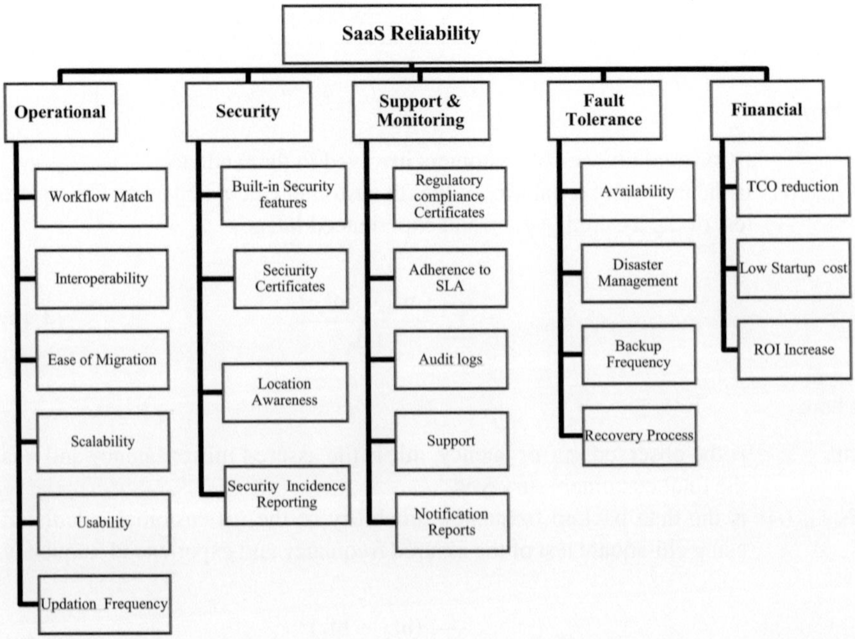

Fig. 4.1 SaaS reliability metric hierarchy

$$R_{\text{recovery}} = \frac{\sum_{i=1}^{n} \text{EFF}_{\text{rec}}(i)}{n}, \tag{4.52}$$

where

n denotes the number of customers surveyed
$\text{EFF}_{\text{rec}}(i)$ is the efficiency of recovery of ith customer which is calculated as

$$\text{EFF}_{\text{rec}} = \binom{n}{x} p^x (1-p)^{n-x},$$

where

n stands for the total number of recovery processes done
x stands for the number of successful recovery processes
p is the probability of the successful recovery which is 0.5

SaaS specific reliability metrics and the common metrics are to be evaluated to compute reliability of a SaaS product. Some of the metrics specific to IaaS and PaaS are also considered in listing of all SaaS metrics as SaaS implementations are done using IaaS and PaaS assistance. The metrics collection is further grouped based on its functionality. Figure 4.1 shows the SaaS metric hierarchy. Likewise the metrics of IaaS and PaaS can also be categorized.

4.6 Summary

This chapter has detailed the cloud reliability metrics. Some of the metrics, such as availability, security, regulatory compliance, incidence reporting adherence to SLA, etc., are common for all the three service models. The metric specific to each service model such as IaaS, PaaS, and SaaS have been discussed in detail. Quantification details for these metrics have been explained for the measurement purpose. Quantification method varies based on the type of users from whom the metric values are to be gathered. Three types of users mentioned are the, (a) customers or developers who are planning to opt for the cloud services, (b) customers or developers who are already using the cloud application or services and (c) the cloud brokers who keep track of the cloud standards and cloud service operations. A 360° view covering all the characteristics of cloud reliability evaluation has been presented in this chapter.

References

BizTechReport. (2010). *Online business continuity solutions for small businesses—Comparison report. A solution for small business report series*. Retrieved October 5, 2013 from www.BizTechReports.com.

Brussels. (2014). *Cloud service level agreement standardization guidelines*. Retrieved March 20, 2015 from http://ec.europa.eu/information_society/newsroom/cf/dae/document.cfm?action=display&doc_id=6138.

Cloud Standards Customer Council. (2015). *Practical guide to platform-as-a-service, a guide, Version 1.0*. September, 2015 article retrieved on November, 2017 from www.cloud-council.org/CSCC-Practical-Guide-to-PaaS.pdf.

Cloud Standards Customer Council. (2017). *Interoperability and portability for cloud computing: A guide Version 2.0*. http://www.cloud-council.org/CSCC-Cloud-Interoperability-and-Portability.pdf.

Garg, S. K., Versteeg, S., & Buyya, R. (2013). A framework for ranking cloud computing services. *Journal of Future Computer Generation Systems, 29*(4), 1012–1023.

GeSI. (2013). *Greenhouse gas protocol: Guide for assessing GHG emission of cloud computing and data center services*. Retrieved May 15, 2015 from http://www.ghgprotocol.org/files/ghgp/GHGP-ICT-Cloud-v2-6-26JAN2013.pdf.

Kumar, V., & Vidhyalakshmi, P. (2013). SaaS as a business development tool. In *Conference Proceedings of International Conference on Business Management (ICOBM, 2013), University of Management and Technology, Lahore, Pakistan*.

Marja & Matt. (2002). *Exploring usability enhancement in W3C process*. Retrieved March, 2013 from https://www.w3.org/2002/Talks/0104-usabilityprocess/Overview.html.

Rosenberg, L., Hammer, T., & Shaw, J. (1998). Software metrics and reliability. In *9th International Symposium on Software Reliability Engineering*.

Rouse, M. (2016). *Cloud disaster recovery (cloud DR)*. Retrieved April, 2017 from https://searchdisasterrecovery.techtarget.com/definition/cloud-disaster-recovery-cloud-DR.

Stanton, B., Theofanos, M., & Joshi, K. P. (2014). Framework for cloud usability. In Human Aspects of Information Security, Privacy and Trust (pp. 664–671). Springer International Publishing.

Singh, J., & Kumar, V. (2013). *Compliance and regulatory standards for cloud computing. A volume in IGI global book series advances in e-business research (AEBR)*. https://doi.org/10.4018/978-1-4666-4209-6.ch006.

Tech Target Whitepaper. (2015). Regaining control of the cloud. *Information Security, 17*(8). Retrieved October 3, 2015 from www.techtarget.com.

Vidhyalakshmi, R., & Kumar, V. (2016). Determinants of cloud computing adoption by SMEs. *International Journal of Business Information Systems, 22*(3), 375–395.

Zeifman, I. (2015). *12 tips for choosing data center location*. Retrieved April, 2017 from https://www.incapsula.com/blog/choosing-data-center-location.html.

Chapter 5
Reliability Model

Abbreviations

AHP	Analytic Hierarchy Process
CORE	Customer-Oriented Reliability Evaluation
MADM	Multiattribute Decision-Making
MCDM	Multicriteria Decision-Making
MODM	Multiobjective Decision-Making
RE	Reliability Evaluators
SME	Small and Medium Enterprises

Having discussed the reliability metrics of all cloud service models, such as IaaS, PaaS and SaaS in detail, let us move on to reliability evaluation. In this chapter, we will discuss how various metrics are combined and evaluated. *Customer-Oriented Reliability Evaluation* (CORE) model has been presented to evaluate the reliability of cloud services. This model is based on Analytic Hierarchy Process (AHP), which is one of the Multicriteria Decision-Making (MCDM) techniques. Due to the hierarchical nature of the metrics and reliability being user-oriented, AHP method is chosen. A structured research instrument is used to gather information from the customers. Based on the business requirements, the customers have to fill out this questionnaire. This is used to calculate the priority for the metrics. User of the CORE model should be a person with sound knowledge of cloud technology and services. It can be either the customer or a cloud broker. The model evaluates reliability attributes for the cloud products and stores them in the model. Customer priorities and periodically stored reliability metric values are used by AHP to provide a single final numeric value between 0 and 1. The model is designed to provide a single value for the product as well as a comparative ranking of multiple products based on its reliability value.

V. Kumar and R. Vidhyalakshmi, *Reliability Aspect of Cloud Computing Environment*, https://doi.org/10.1007/978-981-13-3023-0_5

5.1 Introduction

Reliability metrics for all the service models such as IaaS, PaaS, and SaaS were discussed in detail in the previous chapter. Final reliability value has to be computed from these metrics. We have already discussed in detail in Chap. 2, that reliability is user-oriented. Hence, not all metrics will be of equal importance. The priorities for the reliability metrics will vary with the business requirements of the customers. For example, security is considered as an important factor for the financial organization but the same may be of less importance for any academic setup. Multiple platform provisioning is of prime importance for academic users but the same is not of any importance for any Small and Medium Enterprises (SME) who are adopting cloud services for their business operations. Due to this variance, the factor ranking cannot be standardized and also ranking of the reliability factors based on the user priority is essential.

The presence of multiple metrics with varying importance depending on business requirement and the complexity involved in the metrics representation excludes the use of traditional methods for reliability evaluation. Conventional methods such as weighted sum or weighted product based methods are avoided and Multiple-Criteria Decision-Making (MCDM) methods are used. MCDM is a subfield of operations research that utilizes mathematical and computational tools to assist in making decisions in the presence of multiple quantifiable and nonquantifiable factors. There are numerous categories of MCDM methods and of all, Analytic Hierarchy Process (AHP) is chosen due to the categorization of the reliability metrics in hierarchical format.

A model named Customer-Oriented Reliability Evaluation (CORE) (Vidhyalakshmi and Kumar 2017) is explained in this chapter, which will help customers to calculate the reliability of the cloud services that are chosen. The user of the model should be a person with sound knowledge of cloud services and its technology. It could be the customer or a broker. When customers are naïve to cloud usage, then broker-based method can be used. The brokers are also termed as *Reliability Evaluators* (RE). The role of the REs is to provide guidance to customers and educate them about the following:

i. Streamline business processes to meet global standards
ii. Features to look for in any cloud services
iii. Risk mitigations measures
iv. Ways to prioritize reliability metrics
v. Monitoring of cloud services
vi. Standards and certifications required for compliance

The CORE model has three layers: User Preference Layer, Reliability Evaluation Layer, and Repository Layer. All the standards and usage-based metric defined in Chap. 3 under Sect. 3.4 are calculated for popular cloud products and are stored in the Repository Layer. The customer preferences are evaluated as metric priorities and are stored in User Preference Layer. The priorities and metric values are used by the middle layer (i.e.) Reliability Evaluation Layer to arrive at final reliability value. These calculated values are also time stamped and stored in the repository layer. This will help to identify the growth of the cloud service or product over a period of time.

The CORE model will be helpful for the cloud users and cloud service providers. The cloud users can identify reliable cloud product that suits their business. Naïve users will get a chance to streamline business process to meet global standards and enhance web presence. The customers will also get knowledge about what to expect from an efficient cloud product. The existing users of cloud are benefitted by the model implementation as it will enable them to monitor the performance which is essential to keep the operational cost under control. The CORE model will also assist Cloud Service Providers in many ways. Interaction with Reliability Evaluators will assist the providers to gain an insight of the customer requirements. This will assist providers to enhance the product features which will result in enhanced product quality and customer base. Some of the other benefits for the service providers are

i. Enhancement of their product.
ii. Creation of healthy competition among the providers.
iii. Keeping track of their product performance.
iv. Know the position of their product in the market.
v. To gain information about the performance of the competitors' products.

5.2 Multi Criteria Decision Making

Multi Criteria Decision Making (MCDM) is a branch of a general class of operations research models. It deals with decision problems to be undertaken with numerous decision criteria. The traditional method of single criteria decision-making concentrates mainly on efficient option selection for maximizing benefits by minimizing cost. The globalization process, environmental awareness, and technology developments have increased the complexity of decision-making. The MCDM usage in these scenarios improves the decision-making process by providing an evaluation of the features involved in the decision-making, promoting the involvement of participants in decision-making and understanding the perception of models' in real-world scenario (Pohekar and Ramachandran 2004).

MCDM is further categorized as Multi Objective Decision-Making (MODM) and Multi Attribute Decision-Making (MADM) based on the usage of alternatives (Climaco 1997). These categories have various other methods such as distance based, outranking, priority based, mixed methods, etc. These methods can further be classified based on the nature of decision-making as deterministic, fuzzy, and stochastic methods. Decision-making methods can also be classified as single or group decision-making based on the number of users involved in the decision-making process (Gal and Hanne 1999).

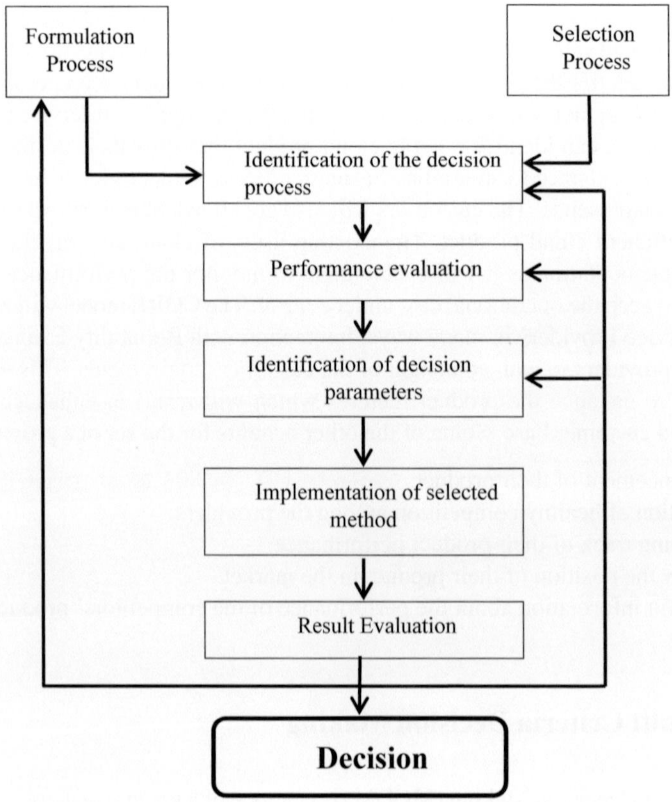

Fig. 5.1 Multicriteria decision-making process

These MCDM methods have common characteristics such as incomparable units for criteria, conflicts among criteria, and difficulties in choosing from alternatives. The MODM method does not have predetermined alternatives instead optimized objective functions are identified based on set of constraints. MADM has predefined alternatives and a subset is evaluated against a set of attributes. Figure 5.1 depicts the various steps involved in Multicriteria Decision-Making process.

5.2.1 Types of MCDM Methods

Various methods used in MCDM are weighted sum, weighted product, Analytic Hierarchy Process (AHP), preference ranking organization method for enriching evaluation, Elimination and Choice Translating Reality (ELECTRE), Multiattribute Utility Theory (MAUT), Analytical Network Process, goal programming, fuzzy, Data Envelopment Analysis (DEA), Gray Relation Analysis (GRA), etc (Whaiduzzaman et al. 2014). All these methods share common characteristics of divergent criteria, difficulty in the selection of alternatives and unique units. These methods are solved using evaluation matrix, decision matrix, and payoff matrix. Some of the MCDM methods are discussed below.

i. Multi Attribute Utility Theory: The preferences of the decision maker are accepted in the form of a utility function that is defined for a set of factors. Preferences are given in the scale of 0–1 with 0 being the worst preference and 1 being the best. The utility functions are separated by addition or multiplication utility functions with respect to single attribute (Keeny and Raiffa 1976).
ii. Goal Programming: This is a branch of multiobjective optimization. It is a generalization of linear programing techniques. It is used to achieve goals subjected to the dynamically changing and conflicting objective constraints with the help of modifying slack and few other variables that represents deviation from the goal. Unwanted deviations from a collection of target values are minimized. It is used to determine the resources required, degree of goal attainment, and provide best optimal solution under dynamically varying resources and goal priorities (Scniederjans 1995).
iii. Preference Ranking Organization Method for Enrichment Evaluation:- This method is abbreviated as PROMETHEE. This method uses outranking principle to provide priorities for the alternatives. Ranking is done based on the pair wise comparison with respect to the number of criteria. It provides best suitable solution rather than providing the right decision. Six general criterion functions such as Gaussian criterion, level criterion, quasi criterion, usual criterion, criterion with linear preference and criterion with linear preference and indifference area are used (Brans et al. 1986).
iv. Elimination and Choice Translating Reality: ELECTRE is the abbreviation for this method. Both qualitative and qualitative criteria are handled by this method. Best alternative decision is chosen from most of the criteria. Concordance index, discordance index, and threshold values are used and based on the indices graphs for strong and weak relationships are developed. Iterative procedures are applied for the graphs to get the ranking of the alternatives (Roy 1985).

5.3 Analytical Hierarchy Process

AHP discovered by Thomas L. Satty is used in this research for the quantification of factors as it the suitable method to be used for qualitative and quantitative factors and for the pair wise comparisons of factors arranged in hierarchical order.

It is a method that utilizes the decision of experts to derive the priority of the factors and calculates the measurement of alternatives using pair wise comparisons. The complex problem of decision-making, involving various factors is decomposed into clusters and pair wise factor comparisons are done within the cluster. This

Table 5.1 Absolute number scale used for factor comparison

Scale value	Description
1	Factor being compared have equal importance
2, 3	A factor has weak or slight moderate importance over another
4, 5	A factor has moderate plus strong dominance over another factor
6, 7	A factor if favored very strongly over another
8	A factor has very, very strong dominance over another
9	The factor has extreme importance over the other factors

enables the decision-making problems to be solved easily with less cognitive load. The following steps are followed in AHP (Satty 2008):

i. Examine the problem and identify the aim of decision.
ii. Build the decision hierarchy with the goal at the top of the hierarchy along with the factors identified at the next level. The intermediate levels are filled with the compound factors with the lowest level of the hierarchy having the atomic measurable factors.
iii. Construct the pairwise comparison matrix
iv. Calculate the Eigen vector iteratively to find the ranking of the factors.

The pairwise comparison is done using the scaling of the factors to indicate the importance of a factor over another. This process is done between factors for all the level in the hierarchy. The fundamental scaling used for factor comparison is given in Table 5.1. The cloud users wanting to evaluate the reliability of chosen cloud services should have the clear understanding of their business operations. Based on the requirements the importance of one reliability metric over another has to be provided. The absolute number scale to be used for providing preference is specified in Table 5.1.

5.3.1 Comparison Matrix

This is a square matrix of order as same as the number of factors being compared. Each cell value of the matrix is filled with values depending on the preferences chosen by the customers. The diagonal elements of this matrix are marked as 1. The rest of the elements are filled following the rules given below:

If factor i is five times more important than factor j, then the $CM_{i,j}$ value is 5 and the transpose position $CM_{j,i}$ is filled with its reciprocal value.

Let us take an example of a computer system purchase. Assume Customer A is an end user who has decided to purchase a new computer system for his small business. The factors to be looked for are hardware, software and vendor support. Three systems such as S1, S2, and S3 are shortlisted. Now based on the usage, the factors are to be provided significance based on the numbers mentioned in Table 5.1. The first step

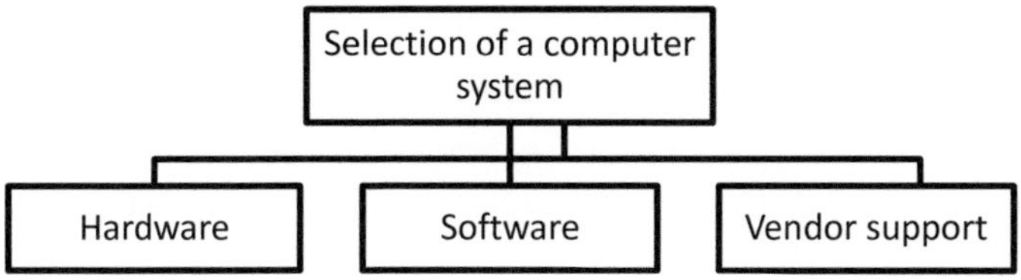

Fig. 5.2 Decision hierarchy

Table 5.2 Comparison matrix example

	Hardware	Software	Vendor support
Hardware	1	1/9	1/3
Software	9	1	3
Vendor support	3	1/3	1

is to design the problem in hierarchical format to have better understanding of the problem. Figure 5.2 shows the hierarchical structure of the problem.

Customer A has decided to give extreme high preference for Software than hardware and moderate preference than vendor support. So, extreme high priority number 9 is assigned for software when compared to hardware and moderate preference number 3 is assigned for software when compared to vendor support. The customer has chosen to given moderate importance to vendor support over hardware. The resulting comparison matrix is given in Table 5.2.

The diagonal element of the matrix is a comparison to itself, which is an equal comparison. Hence 1 is assigned to the diagonal element. Software is 8 time more important than hardware hence 8 is assigned in the intersection of software and hardware. The reciprocal of the same is assigned in the hardware and software intersection. All the fraction values are computed and the final comparison matrix will be

$$\begin{bmatrix} 1 & 0.111 & 0.333 \\ 9 & 1 & 3 \\ 3 & 0.333 & 1 \end{bmatrix}$$

5.3.2 *Eigen Vector*

After the creation of comparison matrix iterations of Eigen vector creation needs to be done. The steps to be followed in the Eigen vector creation are

i. Square the comparison matrix by multiplying the matrix with itself.
ii. Add all the elements of the rows to create the row sum.
iii. Total the row sum values.

iv. Normalize the row sum to create Eigen vector by dividing each row sum with total of row sum. The Eigen vector is calculated with four digits precision.

The above steps are repeated until the difference between the Eigen vector of the ith iteration and $i-1$th iteration is negligible with respect to four digits precision. The sum of the Eigen vector is 1. The values of the Eigen vector are used to identify the rank or the order of the factors. These are assigned as the weights for the factors of first level and used in final computation of reliability.

Alternate way is

i. Multiply all values of a row and calculate the nth root, where "n" refers to the number of factors.
ii. Find the total of the nth root value.
iii. Normalize each row nth row value by dividing it with the total.
iv. The resulting values are the Eigen vector values.

For the example of computer selection the Eigen vector is calculated as follows:

i. Multiply the comparison matrix with itself. The resultant matrix will be

$$\begin{bmatrix} 1 & 0.111 & 0.333 \\ 9 & 1 & 3 \\ 3 & 0.333 & 1 \end{bmatrix} \times \begin{bmatrix} 1 & 0.111 & 0.333 \\ 9 & 1 & 3 \\ 3 & 0.333 & 1 \end{bmatrix} = \begin{bmatrix} 3 & 0.33333 & 1 \\ 27 & 3 & 9 \\ 9 & 1 & 3 \end{bmatrix}$$

ii. Compute row sum for each row. Calculate the total of the row sum column.

$$\begin{bmatrix} 3 & 0.3333 & 1 \\ 27 & 3 & 9 \\ 9 & 1 & 3 \end{bmatrix} \begin{matrix} 4.3333 \\ 39 \\ 13 \end{matrix}$$

iii. The total of the row sum column is 56.333. This value is used to normalize the row sum column

$$\begin{bmatrix} 3 & 0.3333 & 1 \\ 27 & 3 & 9 \\ 9 & 1 & 3 \end{bmatrix} \begin{matrix} 4.3333 & 0.0769 \\ 39 & 0.6923 \\ 13 & 0.2308 \end{matrix}$$

iv. The last column is the Eigen Vector [0.0769, 0.6923, 0.2308]. This is also called as priority vector. Addition of this vector will be 1. The priority for hardware is 0.0769, software is 0.6923 and that of the vendor support is 0.2308.

5.3.3 Consistency Ratio

After the calculation of Eigen Vector, Consistency Ratio (CR) is calculated to validate the consistency of the decision. The ability to calculate CR sets AHP ahead of other MCDM methods like Goal Programming, Multiattribute Utility Theory, Choice experiment, etc. The four steps of CR calculation are

i. Add the column sum of the comparison matrix. Multiply each column sum with its respective priority value.
ii. Calculate λ_{max} as sum of the multiplied values. λ_{max} value need not be 1.
iii. Consistency Index (CI) is calculated as $(\lambda_{max} - n)/(n - 1)$, where n is the number of criteria.
iv. CR is calculated as CI/RI, where RI is called the Random Index. RI is a direct function based on the number of criteria being used. RI lookup table provided by Thomas L. Satty for 1–10 criteria is given in Table 5.3.

Lower CR value indicates consistent decision-making whereas higher CR value indicates that the decision is not consistent. CR value ≤ 0.01 indicates that the decision is consistent. If the value of CR is >0.01, then decision maker should reconsider the pairwise comparison values.

For the computer selection example the CR values are calculated as follows. Column sum for the comparison matrix is calculated and placed as fourth row.

$$\begin{bmatrix} 1 & 0.111 & 0.333 \\ 9 & 1 & 3 \\ 3 & 0.333 & 1 \\ \mathbf{13} & \mathbf{1.444} & \mathbf{4.3333} \end{bmatrix}$$

The last row is then multiplied with priority values [0.0769, 0.6923, 0.2308] and then added to get λ_{max}.

$\lambda_{max} = [13 * 0.0769 + 1.444 * 0.6923 + 4.333 * 0.2308] = 3.$

Table 5.3 Random Index Lookup table

Criteria number	Random index
1	0.00
2	0.00
3	0.58
4	0.90
5	1.12
6	1.24
7	1.32
8	1.41
9	1.45
10	1.49

CI is calculated as $(\lambda_{max} - n)/(n - 1)$. (i.e.) $(3 - 3)/2 = 0$.
RI for three criteria is 0.58. CR = CI/RI = 0/0.58 = 0.
As CR is <0.1 the comparisons provided are consistent.

5.3.4 *Sample Input for SaaS Product Reliability*

Reliability metrics of all the three models and its hierarchy is defined in Chap. 4. Further in this chapter let us consider metrics for SaaS model and its hierarchy. The pairwise comparison for the metrics and its calculations are shown in this section. As an example, let us assume customer A has a small business setup and is willing to adopt SaaS product. The metrics are explained and the pair wise comparison is accepted for the all the levels of reliability metrics.

a. **First-level metrics**

First level has four metrics such as *Operational, Security, Support and Monitoring, and Fault Tolerance*. The pairwise comparison between them is as follows:

i. *Operational* metrics has strong dominance (8) over *Security*, moderately plus strong dominance (5) over *Support and Monitoring* and *Fault tolerance*.
ii. *Support and Monitoring* and has moderate plus strong dominance (5) over *Security*.
iii. *Fault tolerance* is preferred strongly (7) over *Security* and has moderate plus strong dominance (5) over *Support and Monitoring*

The comparison matrix will be a 4 × 4 matrix as there are four metrics in this level. The values of the pairwise comparison are

	Operational	Security	Support and monitor	Fault tolerance
Operational	1	8	5	5
Security	1/8	1	1/5	1/7
Support and monitor	1/5	5	1	1/5
Fault tolerance	1/5	7	5	1

The comparison matrix for the same is

$$\begin{bmatrix} 1 & 8 & 5 & 5 \\ 0.125 & 1 & 0.2 & 0.1428 \\ 0.2 & 5 & 1 & 0.2 \\ 0.2 & 7 & 5 & 1 \end{bmatrix}$$

On squaring the comparison matrix the resultant product matrix is

$$\begin{bmatrix} 4.000 & 76.000 & 36.600 & 12.142 \\ 0.318 & 4.000 & 1.739 & 0.950 \\ 1.065 & 13.000 & 4.000 & 2.114 \\ 2.275 & 40.600 & 12.400 & 4.000 \end{bmatrix}$$

The row sum of the matrix is calculated

$$\begin{bmatrix} 4.000 & 76.000 & 36.600 & 12.142 \\ 0.318 & 4.000 & 1.739 & 0.950 \\ 1.065 & 13.000 & 4.000 & 2.114 \\ 2.275 & 40.600 & 12.400 & 4.000 \end{bmatrix} \begin{matrix} 128.743 \\ 7.009 \\ 20.179 \\ 59.275 \end{matrix}$$

The addition of the row sum column is 215.206. Priority vector or the Eigen vector for the first-level reliability metrics is achieved by normalizing the row sum with the total value. On dividing the row sum with their total the resulting priority vector is [0.598, 0.033, 0.094, 0.275]. Sum of the Eigen vector is 1. This is the preference for the metrics [Operational, Security, support and monitoring, fault tolerance] respectively.

Next step is to check the Consistency Ratio for the preferences given. The column sum of the comparison matrix is first calculated.

$$\begin{bmatrix} 1.000 & 8.000 & 5.000 & 5.000 \\ 0.125 & 1.000 & 0.200 & 0.142 \\ 0.200 & 5.000 & 1.000 & 0.200 \\ 0.200 & 7.000 & 5.000 & 1.000 \\ \mathbf{1.525} & \mathbf{21.000} & \mathbf{11.200} & \mathbf{6.342} \end{bmatrix}$$

The last highlighted value is the column sum. Calculate λ_{max} by multiplying each column sum with their corresponding priority vector value

$\lambda_{max} = [1.525 * 0.598 + 21.000 * 0.033 + 11.200 * 0.094 + 6.342 * 0.275] = 4.393$.

CI is calculated as $(\lambda_{max} - n)/(n - 1)$. (i.e.) $(4.393 - 4)/3 = 0.1$

RI for four criteria is 0.9. CR = CI/RI = 0.1/0.9 = 0.1

As CR is ≤ 0.1 the pairwise comparisons provided are consistent.

b. **Second level metrics**

Each metric in the first level is further sub-divided. After completion of pairwise comparison of the first-level metrics, the same procedure has to be applied for the next level of metrics. The pairwise comparison of second level of *Operational* metrics is given in Table 5.4. The sub-metrics of operational metrics are

i. Workflow Match
ii. Interoperability
iii. Ease of Migration
iv. Scalability

Table 5.4 Pairwise comparison for operation metrics of a SaaS product

Operational metrics	Importance	Operational metrics
Workflow match	Extreme important (9)	Interoperability
	Strong dominance (8)	Migration
	Favored strongly over (7)	Scalability
	Moderate plus strong dominance over (5)	Usability
	Moderate dominance over (4)	Updation frequency
Interoperability	–	Workflow match
	–	Migration
	–	Scalability
	–	Usability
	–	Updation frequency
Migration	–	Workflow match
	Moderate dominance over (4)	Interoperability
	–	Scalability
	–	Usability
	–	Updation frequency
Scalability		Workflow match
	Strong dominance (8)	Interoperability
	Favored strongly over (7)	Migration
	Slight moderate importance over (3)	Usability
	–	Updation frequency
Usability	–	Workflow match
	Moderate plus strong dominance over (5)	Interoperability
	Favored strongly over (7)	Migration
	–	Scalability
	–	Updation frequency
Updation frequency	–	Workflow match
	Extreme important (9)	Interoperability
	Favored strongly over (7)	Migration
	Moderate plus strong dominance over (5)	Scalability
	Moderate plus strong dominance over (5)	Usability

v. Usability
vi. Updation Frequency

The pairwise comparison should be provided only for the metrics that are favored higher than the other. For example, *Workflow Match* metric is of extreme importance than *Interoperability*, so "9" is mentioned in the table. Pairwise comparison of the reverse is not required (i.e.) comparison between *Interoperability* and *Workflow Match* metrics is not needed as the reciprocal value will be stored. Refer to Sect. 5.3.1 for comparison matrix creation.

The comparison matrix for the above table is

$$\begin{bmatrix} 1.000 & 9.000 & 8.000 & 7.000 & 5.000 & 4.000 \\ 0.111 & 1.000 & 0.250 & 0.125 & 0.2000 & 0.111 \\ 0.125 & 4.000 & 1.000 & 0.142 & 0.142 & 0.142 \\ 0.142 & 8.000 & 7.000 & 1.000 & 3.000 & 0.200 \\ 0.200 & 5.000 & 7.000 & 0.333 & 1.000 & 0.200 \\ 0.250 & 9.000 & 7.000 & 5.000 & 5.000 & 1.000 \end{bmatrix}$$

The Eigen vector for the above matrix is

$$\begin{bmatrix} 0.448 & 0.017 & 0.028 & 0.137 & 0.088 & 0.282 \end{bmatrix}$$

This indicates the priorities assigned for the second level of *Operational* metric. λ_{max} for the above comparison matrix is 6.98. Consistency Index is calculated for 6 metrics as 0.19. The final Consistency Ratio is calculated as 0.15 (Refer Random Index for six metrics from Table 5.3. The value is greater than 0.01. Hence the pairwise comparison is not consistent and needs to be reconsidered.

The *Workflow Match* is essential to maintain dynamism in business. Updation frequency also refers to keep up with the changes. Hence both can be given equal importance (i.e.) 1. On 4 with 1 and recalculating the entire process again the Consistency Ratio will be equal to 0.1, which shows that the comparisons are valid and consistent.

The above given pairwise comparison process has to be done for all the levels of the metrics in the hierarchy and based on the lower level metrics priority the higher level values are further calculated.

5.4 CORE Reliability Evaluation

The reliability evaluation model is named as CORE (Customer-Oriented Reliability Evaluation) model. It works completely based on the customer preferences for the reliability metrics. Various steps involved in this model creation are

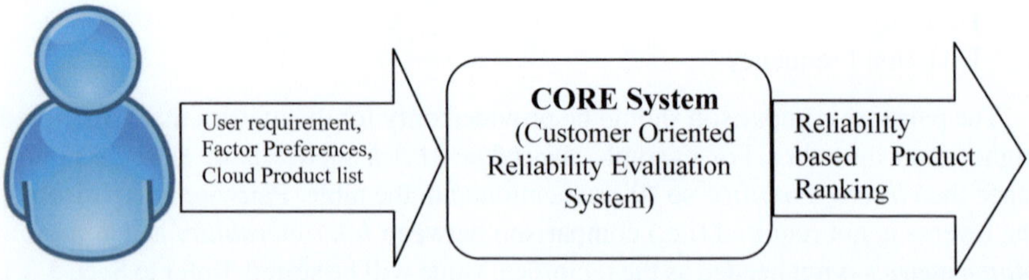

Fig. 5.3 Context diagram of CORE model

1. Identification of metrics and its sub-metrics for the reliability base.
2. Ranking the metrics based on the customer choice
3. Using the numerical formulas for calculating both quantitative and qualitative metrics
4. Calculating the reliability for the product
5. Ranking of the products using relative reliability matrix and relative reliability vector.

The context diagram of CORE, the reliability evaluation model is given in Fig. 5.3. The input to the model is user factor preference and list of cloud service or products chosen for evaluation and the output from the model is a single numeric value for each product chosen indicating total reliability of the products based on customer perspective.

5.4.1 *Layers of the Model*

The working of the CORE model is divided into layers. The three layers of CORE model are User Preference Layer, Reliability Evaluator Layer, and Repository Layer. The container diagram of the CORE model is given in Fig. 5.4 and the detailed component diagram is given in Fig. 5.5.

5.4.1.1 User Preference Layer

This layer consists of user interface, user preference template, product list, rules for preference assignment. This is the base layer through which the customer orientation for the CORE model is achieved. The customer's reliability factor preference input is accepted through a dashboard interface. The rules to be followed in preference assignment are provided as help on demand. The input has to be given by a person with clear understanding of business needs and technology aspects. This is the layer where the user interacts with RE along with the product list to evaluate its reliability. Sample preferences are provided from the factor preference template. On demand

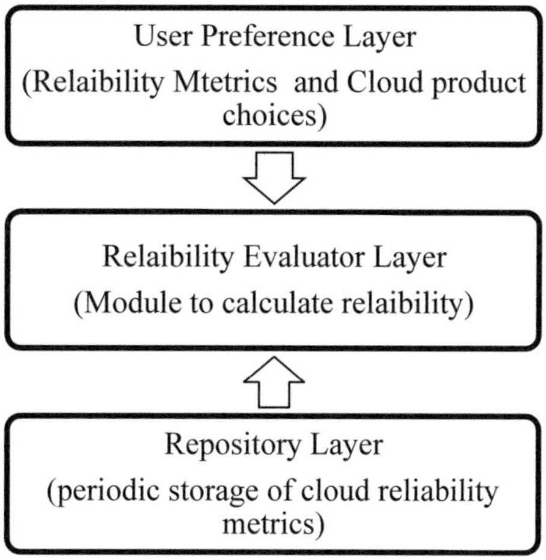

Fig. 5.4 Container diagram of CORE model

Table 5.5 Questionnaire to accept business requirement

Questions	Response type
What are the business requirements to be satisfied by the product?	List of business modules
What are the existing modules that are to be inter operated with the new product	List of modules
What usability requirements are desired in the product?	List of usability requirement
What security certifications are to be maintained by the prospective CSP?	List of security certifications
What compliance certifications are to be maintained by the prospective CSP?	List of compliance certifications
What are the required DR features to be present based on the business needs?	List of DR features

help is provided in case the user does not have any information on products that suit their business needs.

The reliability metrics used and their importance are to be explained to the customers and their preference for the factors is to be accepted. Questionnaire needs to be answered by the prospective customers for gathering details about business requirement.

The questionnaire for a SaaS product selection is given in Table 5.5. The business operations that are to be deployed as cloud services are accepted from the prospective customers as the required functionality or modules and are checked against the modules provided by the shortlisted products. The maximum number of module match count required is accepted from the user. This value will be used in *Workflow Match* sub factor. The list of usability, disaster recovery, security, and compliance specifications are accepted from the customer.

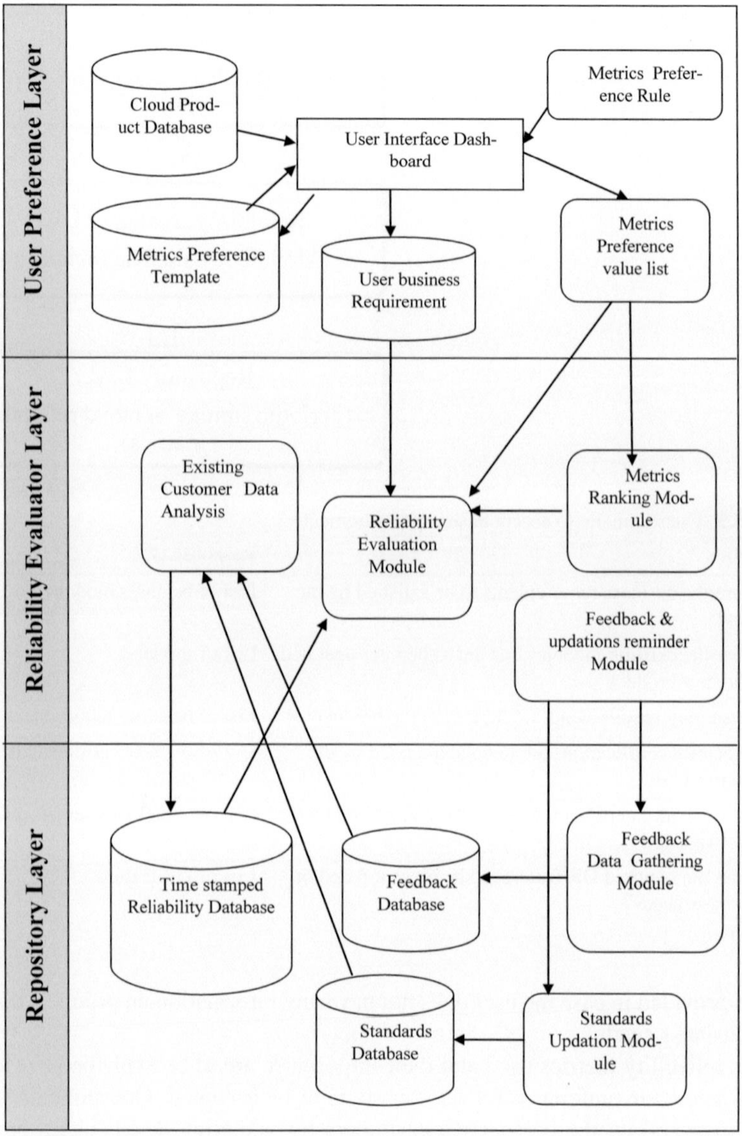

Fig. 5.5 Detailed component diagram of CORE model

5.4.1.2 Reliability Evaluation Layer

This layer is used by the REs who assist customers to find a reliable product for their business operations. Various activities of the REs are customer preference acceptance, reliability calculation, data gathering, and data analysis.

i. Reliability Evaluation

Based on the input from the customer, comparison matrices and Eigen vectors are created for the factor priority identification using AHP technique. The reliability of the atomic metrics is calculated using the calculation method mentioned in Chap. 4. The Relative Reliability Matrix (RRM) is created using the reliability values of the products for each sub factor of level II. The same comparison matrix creation procedure is followed for RRM creation. The corresponding Eigen vector is the Relative Reliability Vector (RRV) of the product for the sub-metrics. These RRVs are then multiplied with the priority values to create the final RRVs for the product. The repetition of this procedure for all the sub-metrics will finally result in a single RRV specifying the reliability ranking of the product.

ii. Data Analysis

The values gathered from the existing customers that are stored in the repository layer are processed as individual factor value for each product. As the data is gathered periodically, the analysis is also carried out periodically. Depending on the type of the reliability metric the evaluation is done using chi-square statistics or cumulative binomial distribution or count based calculations. The calculated values are stored in the repository layer as time stamped reliability database to be used by the reliability evaluation module.

5.4.1.3 Repository Layer

This layer stores various databases used by the CORE model and is the main source for the reliability calculations. The existing customer data and the standards data are gathered and stored in this layer. Due to the huge array of products and its vast customer base, this layer will eventually qualify as big data as the CORE model matures. The basic standard specification of the cloud services are retrieved from the standard specifications laid down by the organizations such as ISO, CSA, CSCC, CoBIT, etc., and these are stored in this layer. These specifications undergo periodic updations which need to be reflected in the repository maintained by the REs. These are utilized in security factor, compliance factor and SLA factor calculations. The existing customer usage details are gathered and the evaluated reliability is stored in the repository layer as time stamped reliability database.

The data from the existing customers need to be gathered at specific interval of time with the help of the survey questionnaire. The questionnaire for SaaS product feedback is given in Table 5.6. As the REs can be approached by customers of any business sector, an extensive collection of data is required with intent to cover the working of majority of the cloud services. These data needs to be stored with time stamp as the increase in customer base will instigate the development of the product. This will eventually result in enhanced performance which will also enhance the reliability of the product. The time stamped data will help to analyze the reliability improvement of the product.

Table 5.6 Existing customer feedback questionnaire

Questions	Response type
Type of business	String
Number of employees working in the organization	Numeric
Business operations for which SaaS products are used along with their names	List
What was the data conversion time assured and actual data conversion time experienced?	Numeric (in minutes)
What was the training time assured and the actual training time observed?	Numeric (in minutes)
How many times scaling was done?	Numeric
How many scaling processes were successful?	Numeric
How many updations were observed in six months?	Numeric
What security features were assured and rendered?	List of features
How many data relocations and how many were within assured places?	Numeric
How many security incidences were reported?	Numeric
What SLOs were rendered accurately?	List of SLOs rendered
Was the log file accessed efficiently?	Boolean
Was the log file retained as specified?	Boolean
How many support calls were made and how many were successful?	Numeric
How many services were responded and how many were responded within time?	Numeric
How many requests were resolved and how many were resolved within the target time?	Numeric
How many notifications were done?	Numeric
What is the observed average availability time for six months?	Numeric
What is the observed mirroring latency?	Numeric (in minutes)
What is the observed backup frequency	Numeric
What is the observed backup retention time?	Numeric (in minutes)
How many recovery processes were done in six months?	Numeric
How many successful recovery processes experienced?	Numeric

The CORE model is completely user-oriented and caters to the business requirements of all types of organizations. The model utilizes factors based on business requirements integrated with the technical components used in SaaS product development. This model generates flexible reliability values for a single SaaS product depending on the business requirement based preferences and hence will be of great use in the pre-SaaS adoption process. MSMEs/SMEs can be benefitted by the implementation of this model as it will enable them to enhance their business process, improve their SaaS product monitoring process and also provides comparative reliability ranking of the selected SaaS product.

5.5 Summary

This chapter has the detailed description about the cloud reliability evaluation. The reliability is user-oriented and has many metrics to consider. Because of this MCDM approach is used instead of traditional weights assigning method. AHP is the chosen MCDM method using which reliability value is calculated. Customer-Oriented Reliability Evaluation (CORE) model is used to evaluate the final reliability value. The model has three layers such as User Preference Layer, Reliability Evaluator Layer, and Repository Layer. End user of the model interacts through User Preference Layer. This layer has templates for the metrics preferences. The entire interaction with the model, like providing cloud product expectation and reliability metrics preference based on business requirement is done in this layer. These inputs are further taken by the reliability evaluator layer which does the final reliability calculations with the help of the Repository Layer of the model. Single cloud product reliability evaluation or comparative ranking of multiple cloud products based on the reliability value is the output of the model.

References

Brans, J. P., Vincke, Ph, & Mareschal, B. (1986). How to select and how to rank projects: The PROMETHEE method. *European Journal of Operations Research, 24,* 228–238.

Climaco, J. (Ed.). (1997). *Multicriteria analysis*. New York: Springer-Verlag.

Gal, T., & Hanne, T. (Eds.). (1999). *Multicriteria decision making: Advances in MCDM models, algorithms, theory, and applications*. New York: Kluwer Academic Publishers.

Keeny, R. L., & Raiffa, H. (1976). *Decisions with multiple objectives: Preferences and value trade-offs*. New York: Wiley.

Pohekar, S. D., & Ramachandran, M. (2004). Application of multi-criteria decision making to sustainable energy planning—A review. *Elsevier Journal of Renewable and Sustainable Energy Review, 8*(4), 365–381.

Roy, B. (1985). *Métodologie multicrite're d'aide la décision. Collection Gestion*. Paris: Economica.

Satty, T. L. (2008). Decision making with analytic hierarchy process. *International Journal of Services Sciences, 1*(1), 83–98.

Scniederjans, M. J. (1995). *Goal programming methodology and applications*. Boston: Kluwer Publishers.

Vidhyalakshmi, R., & Kumar, V. (2017). CORE framework for evaluating the reliability of SaaS products. *Future Generation Computer Systems, 72,* 23–36.

Whaiduzzaman, M., Gani, A., Anuar, N. B., Shiraz, M., Haque, M. N., & Haque, I. T. (2014). Cloud service selection using multicriteria decision analysis. *The Scientific World Journal, 2014*.

Chapter 6
Reliability Evaluation

Abbreviations

CORE	Customer-Oriented Reliability Evaluation
CDF	Cumulative Distribution function
MSME	Micro, Small and Medium Enterprises
RE	Reliability Engineer
RRM	Relative Reliability Matrix
RRV	Relative Reliability Vector
SLA	Service Level Agreement

CORE model explained in Chap. 5 is used to evaluate reliability of the cloud services. Final reliability evaluation can be performed irrespective of the cloud service model. Quality attributes from various standards recommendation is considered as reliability metrics. Hence the model provides 360° view of the reliability perspective. Providing consistent metric preference is essential for successful execution of the model. The model also checks the consistency ratio for each level of metrics preference assignment. SaaS product reliability is chosen for the model explanation in this chapter. The same technique can be applied to identify IaaS and PaaS service reliability. For better understanding of the model working and reliability evaluation, three types of business establishments are taken into consideration. Their metric preferences and business requirements are gathered using questionnaire provided in previous chapter. Step-by-step working of the reliability calculations are explained in detail. This includes individual metric computation, pairwise preference input for metrics and its priority calculations, and final reliability computation. Relative Reliability Matrix (RRM) and Relative Reliability Vectors (RRV) are used to compare the reliability of multiple products. The output of RRV will rank the products based on reliability values.

V. Kumar and R. Vidhyalakshmi, *Reliability Aspect of Cloud Computing Environment*, https://doi.org/10.1007/978-981-13-3023-0_6

6.1 Introduction

The working of Customer-Oriented Reliability evaluation (CORE) model is explained in detail in the following sections of this chapter. The reliability evaluation of SaaS products is explained as an example. The same type of calculation can be applied to the reliability evaluation of products or services of other models such as IaaS and PaaS.

The level of responsibility varies with the service model. Detailed discussion about the accountability for reliability had been discussed in Chap. 2. (Refer Sect. 2.5.3 for further details.) The responsibility of provisioning reliable SaaS product lies with the service provider. But the responsibility of choosing a reliable SaaS product from a huge array of products that are related to their business needs lies with the customer. It is a herculean task as vast array of products are available in the market for a single business function.

Selecting a SaaS product solely based on the tall claims made by the providers is like jumping from the cliff without any height assessment or protection measures. Landing safely after jump will then be a complete luck factor. If luck does not favor, then life will at danger. The SaaS product selection is the same as this. On migration to SaaS, organizations totally depend on it for their operations. Hence it is imperative for the chosen SaaS product to perform without any failure to ensure business continuity. Any deviations from its standard working will eventually end up in financial and customer losses. Exploring the reliability of the product after provisioning them will endanger the business continuity.

A Complete reliability evaluation of a SaaS product must be performed in various aspects like operations, cost, security, resilience etc. Currently there is no statistical method to take the integrated view of SaaS evaluation metrics and to indicate the reliability of a SaaS product in numerical terms.

The reliability evaluation model (CORE) discussed in Chap. 5 is explained with example and the results are analyzed in this chapter. Two MSME customer use cases are discussed in this chapter. These customers are currently using traditional software for accounting operations and are willing to shift to cloud-based accounting SaaS product. Three products are chosen for which the reliability needs to be calculated. On request for anonymity the customers are referred to as C1 and C2 and the product identified for evaluation are referred as P1, P2 and P3 in the rest of this chapter. The feedback pertaining to the working of various SaaS product features are accepted periodically from existing customers by REs and are stored in the repository layer of the model. The data related to the standard security certificates, compliance certificates, SLOs are retrieved from the standards websites by REs and are also stored in the repository layer.

The reliability evaluation process requires input from the existing customers who are currently using the SaaS products and from prospective customers who wants to adopt SaaS product for their operations. One of the important processes of the User Preference Layer of the model is to gather these inputs. The prospective customer input is accepted when they interact with RE for reliability evaluation of the products.

Existing customers' product usage feedback inputs are accepted periodically from numerous customers using surveys and are stored in the repository layer. This is feedback gathering process is carried out product wise and their evaluations are done by the reliability calculation module of the RE layer. These evaluations are stored back in the repository layer for future references.

6.1.1 Assumed Customer Profile Details

Two customers chosen are C1 and C2. They have different business setup and different business requirements but have the same need to computerize accounting.

Profile of Customer C1

Type of business: Designer Textile retailer
Age of business: 4 years
Initial Investment: 20 Lakhs

Customer C1 had rented a shop in the market area and had started had started his business with a single employee. C1's family was helping in garment designing. Manual billing system and book keeping methods were used for accounts operations in the initial years. The business expansion is approximately 25% per year. Now after four years the customer C1 owns a shop, has employed around four people for sales and garment designing processes. MS Excel was being used for monthly and annual accounting operations. With the current IT setup, the customer C1 wants to venture into usage of accounting software. C1 is hesitant to shift to any software for accounting because of the fear that the software usage may insist in the change of business process. The lookout is for such software that suits the business operations.

Profile of customer C2

Type: Stationery retailer
Age of business: 3 years
Initial Investment: 30 Lakhs

Customer C2 had purchased a shop in a shopping complex situated among five educational institutes. Along with stationery, project typing, printing, binding and Xerox facility are also handled. Various computer storage devices and printer cartridges are also sold. Initially two people were employed. Customer C2 being a tech savvy person used electronic billing system and MS-Excel for accounts operations. The business expansion is approximately 35% per year. Currently after 3 years the business has huge customer base and the employee count has increased to 7. The customer with the knowledge of cloud wants to try out cloud application for finance operation. The existing Excel data needs to be moved to the new application and the customer is also willing to mend the business process to suit the software process. Business continuity and security of data is of prime concern for the customer.

The process of using CORE model is as follows:

1. Customer willing to identify reliability of the product approaches the dashboard of the model with the choice of the product or products.
2. The preferences for the metrics and sub-metrics has to be provided by the customer based on the business requirements. If the customer is not able to provide preferences, then help can be availed to display template of preferences by choosing the business type. Help will also be provided to the customers who are naïve to cloud usage. The REs will brief the customers about what to expect from a cloud product or services and guide them to provide preferences.
3. Based on the preferences provided the priority of the metrics and sub-metrics will be calculated.
4. These proprieties are passed on to the next layer which is the reliability Evaluation Layer.
5. Based on the priorities assigned and with the help of the input from the Repository Layer about the past performance of the product and compliance of the product to the standards, the reliability of the chosen product is evaluated. If more than one product is chosen then comparative reliability ranking is also provided by the CORE model.

The detailed reliability calculation process of the metrics and sub-metrics and the final reliability evaluation of the products along with the proof of the model being customer oriented are given in the subsequent sections.

6.2 Reliability Metrics Preference Input

The preference between the metrics and the sub-metrics are accepted from the customers C1 and C2 based on their business requirements. Refer Sect. 5.3.4 for understanding of how to assign comparative preferences for the metrics. The customers will be briefed about the way of preference assignment by Reliability Engineers (REs). If the customers do not have any preference for the metrics, sample preference for the same will be provided. The metrics are compared with other metrics of same level leaving comparison with itself. Hence, the first and the last column of the table is the same. Table 6.1 present first-level metrics preferences of all three customers C1and C2.

Priority calculations are done by creating comparison matrix and Eigen vector as explained in the sub-sections of 5.3. Consistency ratio is also checked as a proof to validate the consistency of the preferences assigned to metrics. If the consistency ration is above 0.1, then the customers are advised to change the preferences. If the customer is not willing to change then the same preferences with consistency ration greater than 0.1 is accepted with a warning. The permissible CR limits are 0.1–0.2 (BPMSG 2017).

The final first-level metric preferences for customer C1 and C2 is given in Table 6.2.

Table 6.1 Comparative preference of first-level metrics

First-level metric	Preference		First-level metrics
	C1	C2	
Operational	8	–	Security
	5	3	Support and monitoring
	5	5	Fault tolerance
Security	–	7	Operational
	–	7	Support and monitoring
		7	Fault tolerance
Support and monitoring	–	–	Operational
	5	–	Security
	–	5	Fault tolerance
Fault tolerance	–	–	Operational
	7	–	Security
	5	–	Support and monitoring

Table 6.2 Priority for first-level metrics

Customer 1		Customer 2	
Metric	Preference	Metric	Preference
Operational	0.60	Operational	0.19
Security	0.03	Security	0.68
Support and monitor	0.09	Support and monitor	0.09
Fault tolerance	0.28	Fault tolerance	0.04

Customer C1 is very particular that the business process should be maintained in the due process of computerization. Hence *operational* metric is given higher preference. Customer C2 being a tech savvy person wants security and business continuity to be maintained. Hence *security* metric is given higher preference as compared to other metrics.

The reliability metrics are provided as a hierarchy. So, each metric defined in Table 6.1 will have subsequent sub-metrics. After completion of the first-level metrics, the second-level metric comparative preferences are accepted from the customers. Table 6.3 lists the comparative preferences of *Operational* metric.

Priority assigned for *operational* sub-metrics are presented in Table 6.4. Customer C1 was very particular about maintaining the business processes. Hence *workflow match* metric is given more importance. Customer C2 on the other hand had system in place and wanted business continuity. Hence Migration is given more preference followed by *Updation Frequency*. Both the customers have placed *updation frequency* metric as the second preferred metric as the SaaS products are preferred over in house application to eliminate the updation and maintenance overhead.

Table 6.3 Comparative preference for *Operational* metrics

Operational sub-metrics	Metrics preference		*Operational* sub-metrics
	C1	C2	
Work flow match	9	3	Interoperability
	8	–	Migration ease
	7	1	Scalability
	5	–	Usability
	4	–	Updation frequency
Interoperability	–	–	Work flow match
	–	–	Migration ease
	–	–	Scalability
	–	–	Usability
	–	–	Updation frequency
Migration Ease	–	7	Work flow match
	4	9	Interoperability
	–	5	Scalability
	–	–	Usability
	–	3	Updation frequency
Scalability	–	–	Work flow match
	8	5	Interoperability
	5	–	Migration ease
	3	3	Usability
	–	–	Updation frequency
Usability	–	3	Work flow match
	5	3	Interoperability
	7	1	Migration ease
	–	–	Scalability
	–	–	Updation frequency
Updation frequency	–	7	Work flow match
	9	7	Interoperability
	7	–	Migration ease
	5	5	Scalability
	5	3	Usability

Table 6.4 Priority for *Operational* metric

Customer 1		Customer 2	
Metric	Preference	Metric	Preference
Work flow match	0.38	Work flow match	0.06
Interoperability	0.02	Interoperability	0.03
Migration	0.03	Migration	0.39
Scalability	0.14	Scalability	0.11
Usability	0.10	Usability	0.12
Updation frequency	0.33	Updation frequency	0.29

Table 6.5 Preferences for *Security* sub-metrics

Security sub-metrics	Metrics preference		Security sub-metrics
	C1	C2	
Built-in features	5	7	Certificates
	9	9	Location awareness
	1	5	Incidence reporting
Certificates	–	–	Built-in features
	7	–	Location awareness
	5	7	Incidence reporting
Location awareness	–	–	Built-in features
	–	7	Certificates
	–	5	Incidence reporting
Incidence reporting	–	–	Built-in features
	–	–	Certificates
	9	–	Location awareness

Table 6.6 Priority for *Security* sub-metrics

Customer 1		Customer 2	
Metric	Preference	Metric	Preference
Built-in features	0.45	Built-in features	0.63
Certificates	0.35	Certificates	0.08
Location awareness	0.03	Location awareness	0.25
Incidence reporting	0.17	Incidence reporting	0.04

Followed by *operational* sub-metric preferences, *security* sub-metrics preferences are accepted from the customers C1 and C2. The sub-metrics of *security* metric are built-in security features, security certificate possession, location awareness feature, and incidence reporting. Table 6.5 lists out the comparative preferences between *security* sub-metrics.

Following comparison matrix creation and Eigen vector calculations, priority for *security* sub-metrics are calculated and are listed in Table 6.6.

Table 6.7 Preferences for *Support and Monitor* sub-metrics

Support and Monitor sub-metrics	Metrics preference		*Support and Monitor* sub-metrics
	C1	C2	
Compliance report	–	–	Adherence to SLA
	3	5	Audit logs
	–	–	Customer support
	3	3	Notification report
Adherence to SLA	3	5	Compliance report
	5	7	Audit logs
	–	1	Customer support
	3	8	Notification report
Audit logs	–	–	Compliance report
	–	–	Adherence to SLA
	–	–	Customer support
	–	–	Notification report
Customer support	3	3	Compliance report
	2	1	Adherence to SLA
	4	6	Audit logs
	3	4	Notification report
Notification report	–	–	Compliance report
	–	–	Adherence to SLA
	3	2	Audit logs
	–	–	Customer support

Table 6.8 Priority for *Support and Monitor* sub-metrics

Customer 1		Customer 2	
Metric	Preference	Metric	Preference
Compliance report	0.17	Compliance report	0.14
Adherence to SLA	0.30	Adherence to SLA	0.44
Audit logs	0.05	Audit logs	0.04
Customer support	0.38	Customer support	0.32
Notification report	0.10	Notification report	0.06

Support and monitoring sub-metrics comparative preferences and priority values are listed in Tables 6.7 and 6.8. The comparative preferences and priority values for *Fault tolerance* sub-metrics are listed in Tables 6.9 and 6.10.

In the above table apart from availability all other metrics are considered as equal by customer C2.

Table 6.9 Preferences for *Fault Tolerance* sub-metrics

Fault Tolerance sub-metrics	Metrics preference		*Fault Tolerance* sub-metrics
	C1	C2	
Availability	9	9	Disaster management
	5	8	Backup frequency
	5	8	Recovery time
Disaster management	–	–	Availability
	–	1	Backup frequency
	–	1	Recovery time
Backup frequency	–	–	Availability
	3	1	Disaster management
	1	1	Recovery time
Recovery time	–	–	Availability
	3	1	Disaster management
	1	1	Backup frequency

Table 6.10 Priority for *Fault Tolerance* sub-metrics

Customer 1		Customer 2	
Metric	Preference	Metric	Preference
Availability	0.65	Availability	0.73
Disaster management	0.05	Disaster management	0.09
Backup frequency	0.15	Backup frequency	0.09
Recovery time	0.15	Recovery time	0.09

After the acceptance of the preferences and calculation of the priority for the metrics, the calculation of the metrics performance has to be done. The SaaS reliability metrics hierarchy with priorities assigned based on the preferences provided by customer C1 is presented in Fig. 6.1.

6.3 Metrics Computation

The value of sub-metrics has to be calculated and combined with the priority values to evaluate reliability of a product. The metrics value of multiple products can be combined in a matrix format from which Eigen vector is calculated. The value of the Eigen vector provides comparative reliability ranking of the products. This is explained in detail in Sect. 6.4.

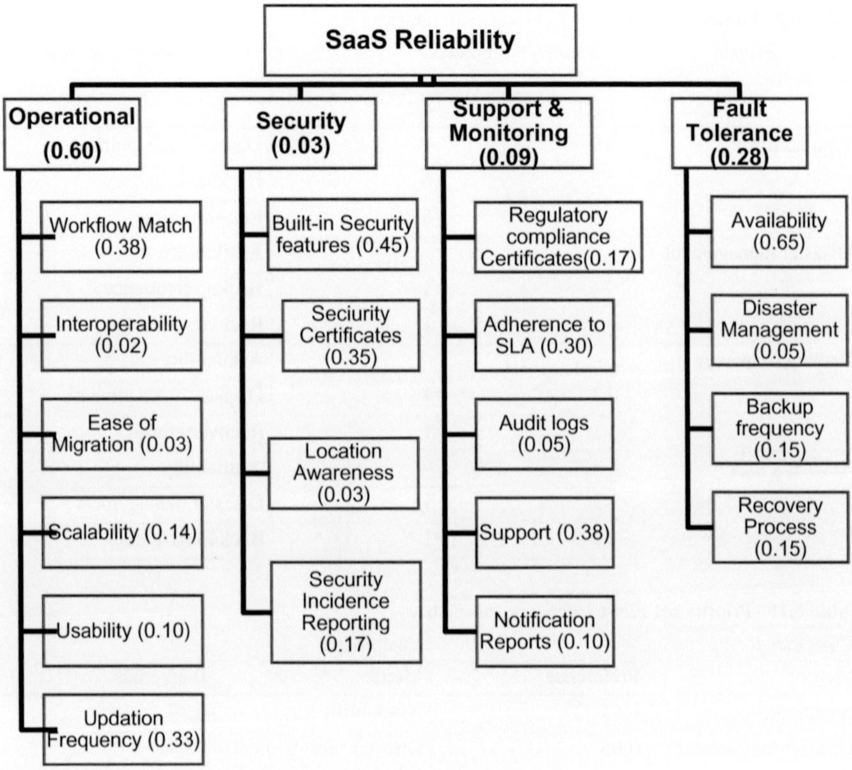

Fig. 6.1 Priorities assigned for the metrics by Customer C1

The lowest level sub-metrics of the reliability metrics hierarchy has to be calculated first. Depending on the type of metrics, the calculation happens at the time of reliability evaluation or calculated periodically and stored in the Repository Layer of the CORE model.

The metrics based on the input from the expectation of the customer who is going to choose the product or services is calculated at the time of reliability evaluation. The metrics based on the feedback from the existing customers are calculated at regular intervals and are stored in the repository layer. The metrics based on the standards are updated periodically based on reminders. The computation of these metrics are also done periodically and stored in the repository layer of the model. The following sections explain all three types of metrics computation.

6.3.1 Expectation-Based Input

This metric is used to accept input from the users who are planning to adopt SaaS product for their business operations. Table 5.5 of Chap. 5 lists out the questionnaire to be used for accepting input from the customers. This has to be filled by customers who have complete knowledge of business and also have knowledge related to cloud usage. Filling this questionnaire will also provide a platform for unorganized business sector customers to streamline their business operations. These metrics are used to evaluate performance of the product which will further be used to calculate the product reliability. These values are calculated like percentage calculations.

If 10 features are expected to be present in a product and all ten are present then the reliability of the product is 1. If 8 features are present, then the reliability of the product is $8/10 = 0.8$.

6.3.2 Usage-Based Input

This input is accepted from the existing users of SaaS product. This calculation gives assurance that the product is delivered as per the catalog specifications.

SaaS product usage feedback of various products is accepted from existing customers and stored in the repository layer. The feedback is obtained using survey which contains questionnaire about the performance of the product. Refer Table 5.6 of Chap. 5 for SaaS product usage questionnaire. The target population is the SaaS products users and the study population for the survey is MSME customers whom have migrated to cloud with or without existing IT infrastructure. Stratified sampling technique is used as the MSMEs are already classified as micro, small and medium enterprises, which are then further classified into various sectors based on the type of industry or services. The customers are divided into "strata" depending on the size and type of business. Each stratum is considered as independent sub-population and samples are randomly selected. The preferred person for the feedback must be IT personnel of the organization who has complete information about the control and monitoring processes of the cloud applications. Panel sampling technique is also included after six months of the CORE model usage in which the same group of existing customers will be surveyed several times over a period of six months. The same strata will be surveyed periodically as the product maturity takes place with time which enhances the reliability. The periodic execution of the existing customer feedback module is used to survey the new customers using stratified sampling along with the old customer's repetitive survey using panel sampling.

Few challenges faced during the feedback accepting process are

i. List of the customers who are using the SaaS products were to be accepted from the SaaS providers. They were reluctant to give the list as they claimed that their product is reliable. They were encouraged to use the model as it will provide the reliability comparison of their product with their competitor's product. It was

Table 6.11 Assured availability hours for products

Product (P1)	Product (P2)	Product (P3)
680	700	710
678	698	705
664	710	719
650	703	715
679	705	719
683	700	716
680	712	719
679	701	715
662	700	719
684	705	719

explained to them that this model will also help them in their product promotion and enhance their customer base. They were assured that the survey results will be shared with them which will also help them to streamline the short comes if any.

ii. Majority of the SaaS product users were not performing exact time-based monitoring of the SaaS operations. The users were briefed about the importance of monitoring the operations. They were explained about the significance of SaaS product reliability for their business operations and the importance of their role in the proposed reliability model. Various factors of the CORE model that are to be monitored and noted down along with the monitoring procedures are explained to the product users. These users were visited after three months to collect their feedback.

The reliability calculation of these metrics based on user feedback is done using Chi-Square method or using Cumulative Distribution Function (CDF) for the binomials. Detailed explanation for the same is available in Sect. 3.5.2. The SaaS reliability sub-metrics like availability, support hours, response time, backup retention, location awareness, ease of migration, updation frequency, etc., are calculated using goodness of fit test. The assured values of these metrics are retrieved from the SLA and the actual provided values are accepted from the existing users of the product. Table 6.11 lists example data for observed availability hours of product P1, P2, and P3. The successive reliability value calculations are listed below the table. The performance of the product with respect to availability is calculated using goodness of fit method due to the presence of expected and observed values.

Product P1 has assured availability of 95%, product P2 has assured availability of 99% and product P3 has assured 99.99% availability. Based on this the expected availability hours for the product availability has to be calculated as follows:

Number of hours in a month = 24 * 60 = 720 h.
Availability hours for Product P1 with 95% assurance = 720 * 95% = **684 h**
Availability hours for Product P2 with 99% assurance = 720 * 99% = **712.8 h**
Availability hours for Product P3 with 99.99% assurance = 720 * 99.99% = **719.28 h**

Table 6.12 Sample calculations of product P1

Observed availability hours	$(\text{Observed—expected})^2$ Expected for P1 = 684	$\frac{(\text{Ob. value}-\text{Exp. value})^2}{\text{Expected Value}}$
680	16	0.023
678	36	0.052
664	400	0.584
650	1156	1.69
679	25	0.036
683	1	0.001
680	16	0.023
679	25	0.036
662	484	0.707
684	0	0.000

The values provided in Table 6.11 are the observed availability of the product collected for a month from 10 different existing customers. Difference between the observed and the expected value for products P1, P2, and P3 is calculated for each customer. The difference is squared and divided by the expected value. Sum of these squared differences is the chi-square value (χ^2). The higher chi-square value indicates more deviation from the assurance provided. The probability of chance occurrence for a given χ^2 value can be calculated from the chi-square calculators available online. Sample calculations for a single product P1 is given in Table 6.12.

Sum of the last column is 3.15 which are slightly on the higher side. This indicates the availability hours provided by the product has some deviation from assured hours. The probability of the χ^2 value calculated from online calculator is 0.957 which also indicates the performance of the product. The same procedure needs to be followed for the chi-square evaluation of the sub-metrics.

If the feedback value for a metric is a dichotomous value like "Yes/No", then cumulative distribution for the binomial functions method is used. The probability of success or failure to deliver the assured services for a product is considered as 0.5 each. The number of trials is the number of occurrences of the event and number of success is the number of times the product has performed as per the specification. For example, audit log metric is calculated based on the successful log access and retention activity. The input accepted from the user is "Yes" or "No" based on the log activity access at the time of need. The count of customers who have answered "yes" will provide the value for the successful event. The number of customers surveyed will be the number of trials. Appling this in the formula as explained in Sect. 3.5.2 we get the performance of the metric. Performance calculation of audit log metric is discussed below.

If ten customers are being surveyed for products P1, P2 and P3, then number of trials = 10.

If 8 customers have answered "Yes" as a mark of successful log access for product 1, then number of successes is 8 and the probability of success and failure is 0.5. Applying all these values in the CDF formula the result is 0.9892. This value indicates the audit log efficiency of product P1.
If five customers have provided "yes" for successful log access, then the CDF calculation with 10 as number of trials and success probability as 0.5 is 0.623.

6.3.3 Standards-Based Input

Standards based inputs are accepted by the Reliability Engineers (REs) at regular intervals and are stored in the repository layer of the model. These standard details have to be updated periodically by REs. The standards based sub-metrics are calculated using Type III metric formulation as explained in Sect. 3.4.1. The reliability value for each sub-metric is calculated as

$$\frac{\text{Number of Standard certificates possessed by the organization}}{\text{Number of certificates suggessted by the standard organization}} \tag{6.1}$$

i. Regulatory Compliance Certificates
Various regulatory compliance certificates need to be maintained to win the customer trust and even to use standard platforms to host SaaS products. Compliance certificates such as

SOC2 → designed specifically as a proof to ensure trust on data storage of a SaaS product.
GDPR → General Data Protection Regulation is designed to harmonize data across Europe. It enforces highest penalty on breach of this compliance.
HIPAA → applies to organizations working with health care. It deals with privacy and security provisions to protect individual's health data.

ii. Disaster Recovery measures
These are the standards that have to be followed to maintain business continuity. Even though organizations should have their own risk mitigation measures with respect to IT usage, it is the responsibility of the SaaS service provider to assure availability of services at the time of need.

ISO 27031 → this has to be possessed by the SaaS companies as a proof that the business continuity steps are followed.
ISO 22301 → helps organizations to understand and prioritize threats with respect to international standards.

Some of the certificate requirement details are explained above. These certification requirements have to be updated periodically as the standards organizations keep modifying the requirements to meet the changing business needs and growing threats.

If the requirement of the certificates is five and the SaaS company possesses 3, then the reliability of the company with respect to certificates is 3/5 = 0.6. If all the required certificates are possessed by the company then the reliability is 1.

6.4 Comparative Reliability Evaluation

If multiple products are chosen for reliability evaluation, then relative ranking of the products is done based on their computed performance values. Metric value computation for each product is done and stored in the Reliability Evaluation layer or Repository Layer depending on its type. Relative weighing method is used to form Relative Reliability Matrix (RRM) from which Relative Reliability Vectors (RRV) are computed to rank the products.

6.4.1 Relative Reliability Matrix

RRM which is Relative Reliability Matrix is used to compare the reliability of chosen products and to calculate the ranking of them based on their performance values. This is a square matrix like comparison matrix with order $N \times N$. Here, N is the number of products being compared. The diagonal elements of this matrix are 1 and the cell value will have the result of the division of comparing row product performance value by the column product performance value.

Let us see the RRM for *workflow match* metrics of product P1, P2, and P3. To create RRM, first the performance value of metric has to be calculated. *Workflow match* is a type I metric. (Refer Sect. 3.5 for metric types and its calculation methods.)

Assume customer C1 has requirement of 10 functionalities in a SaaS product and the requirement matching of product P1, P2, and P3 are given below.

P1 has 8 functionality that match with the requirement so 8/10 = 0.8
P2 has 9 matching required finalities = 9/10 = 0.9
P3 matches all the required functionalities hence 10/10 = 1

Now RRM of the *workflow match* metric will be a 3 × 3 matrix as three products are being compared. Diagonal element of RRM will always be 1 as the product performance is compared with itself.

$$\begin{array}{cccc} & P1(0.8) & P2(0.9) & P3(1) \\ P1(0.8) & 1 & 0.8/0.9 & 0.8/1 \\ P2(0.9) & 0.9/0.8 & 1 & 0.9/1 \\ P3(1) & 1/0.8 & 1/0.9 & 1 \end{array}$$

The resulting matrix will be

$$\begin{bmatrix} 1 & 0.8889 & 0.8000 \\ 1.1250 & 1 & 0.9000 \\ 1.1250 & 1.1111 & 1 \end{bmatrix} \tag{6.2}$$

6.4.2 *Relative Reliability Vector*

Eigen vector computation steps are followed and Relative Reliability Vector is calculated. The RRM is squared and row sums are calculated. The row sum values are normalized to create RRV. The resulting vector is the comparative reliability values of the products.

Creation of RRV from the RRM explained in above Sect. 6.4.1 is given below. The matrix is the resultant product matrix of RRM squaring.

$$\begin{bmatrix} 3.000 & 2.667 & 2.400 \\ 3.375 & 3.000 & 2.700 \\ 3.750 & 3.333 & 3.000 \end{bmatrix}$$

Row sum of each row has to be calculated followed by the total of the row sum value.

$$\begin{bmatrix} 3.000 & 2.667 & 2.400 \\ 3.375 & 3.000 & 2.700 \\ 3.750 & 3.333 & 3.000 \end{bmatrix} \begin{matrix} 8.066 \\ 9.075 \\ 10.083 \end{matrix}$$

Total of row sum column is 27.225. Normalize the values by dividing each row sum with the total 27.225. The resulting vector is RRV which is also the comparative ranking of the products P1, P2, and P3.

$$\begin{bmatrix} 8.066/27.225 & 9.075/27.225 & 10.083/27.225 \end{bmatrix}$$

This when computed will result in RRV = [0.30, 0.33, 0.37]. Product P3 is ranked first among three products. These values are further used along with its priorities for reliability calculation.

Sample data for all SaaS metrics is provided in annexure I. Few metrics value computation followed by its RRM and RRV for all three types of SaaS metrics is given below.

Type I SaaS metric

Disaster management metric is a type I metric. This works with number of DR features required for a product. Depending on the business requirement and IT technical strength of the company the need of DR features varies. Assume customer C1 requires five DR features.

Product P1 satisfies four hence 4/5 = 0.8
Product P2 has three and half features = 3.5/5 = 0.7
Product P3 has almost all but a few slight issues hence 4.5/5 = 0.9

Based on these three values RRM and RRV computations are done as follows:

$$\begin{array}{cccc} & P1(0.8) & P2(0.7) & P3(0.9) \\ P1(0.8) & 1 & 0.8/0.7 & 0.8/0.9 \\ P2(0.7) & 0.7/0.8 & 1 & 0.7/0.9 \\ P3(0.9) & 0.9/0.8 & 0.7/0.9 & 1 \end{array}$$

The final matric after calculation of fractions is

$$\begin{bmatrix} 1 & 1.142 & 0.889 \\ 0.875 & 1 & 0.778 \\ 1.125 & 1.286 & 1 \end{bmatrix}$$

The product matrix after squaring and row sum of each row is

$$\begin{bmatrix} 3.000 & 3.428 & 2.667 \\ 2.625 & 3.000 & 2.333 \\ 3.375 & 3.857 & 3.000 \end{bmatrix} \begin{array}{c} 9.09 \\ 7.95 \\ 10.23 \end{array}$$

Total of row sum column is 27.28. RRV after normalizing row sum values is [0.33, 0.292, 0.375].

Type II SaaS metric

Location awareness is a sub-metric of *security* metric. Some customers of healthcare or finances sector will be very much concerned about the safety of their customer's data. They will be very specific about hosting location of their data. Many cloud service providers also provide choice for customers to select their data center locations. The movement of the data from one location to another for whatsoever reason must be conveyed to the customer. This increases security transparency for the data. Performance of this metric is computed using type II metric calculation method. (Refer Sect. 3.5 for type II metric calculation method.) The information such as number of data movement to chosen location and total number of data movements in a span of 3 months are collected from existing customers. The efficiency value is calculated as (no. of data movements to chosen locations/total number of data movements). Table 6.13 shows sample data of ten customers.

The RRM created using the values of *location awareness* metrics is

Table 6.13 Location awareness data of product P1

No. of data movements to chosen location			Total number of data movements			Efficiency of location awareness		
P1	P2	P3	P1	P2	P3	P1	P2	P3
7	9	6	9	9	6	0.7778	1	1
5	8	7	5	8	7	1	1	1
9	5	5	10	5	6	0.9	1	0.833
4	6	6	4	6	6	1	1	1
7	6	5	8	7	5	0.875	0.857	1
9	8	6	12	8	6	0.75	1	1
5	5	6	7	5	7	0.714	1	0.857
6	7	7	6	9	8	1	0.777	0.875
7	8	7	7	8	7	1	1	1
3	9	6	3	10	6	1	0.9	1
Average efficiency value						0.901	0.953	0.956

$$\begin{bmatrix} 1 & 0.945 & 0.942 \\ 1.057 & 1 & 0.996 \\ 1.060 & 1.003 & 1 \end{bmatrix}$$

The product of squaring RRM along with its row sum is

$$\begin{bmatrix} 3.000 & 2.837 & 2.828 \\ 3.172 & 3.000 & 2.990 \\ 3.182 & 3.009 & 3.000 \end{bmatrix} \begin{matrix} 8.665 \\ 9.162 \\ 9.192 \end{matrix}$$

The total of row sum is 27.01. RRV after normalizing each row sum is [0.32, 0.34, 0.34]

Type II SaaS metric

These types of metrics are calculated based on the standards recommended by the organizations like ISO, CSMIC, SMI, etc. All cloud products and services are expected to follow these standards. Customers also expect the presence of standards as per their business requirements. Refer Sect. 3.5 for detailed understanding of Type III metrics calculation.

Let us take *security certificates* metrics as an example. Assume based on the business security requirements, customer C1 lists out that five security certificates are essential for choosing the product.

Product P1 has three certificates hence 3/5 = 0.6
Product P2 has four certificates hence 4/5 = 0.8
Product P3 contains all the required certificates. Hence 5/5 = 1

Security certificates metric values 0.6, 0.8 and 1 of the products P1, P2 and P3 are used to calculate RRM and RRV as explained above.

RRM using metric values is

$$\begin{bmatrix} 1 & 0.666 & 0.600 \\ 1.500 & 1 & 0.900 \\ 1.667 & 1.111 & 1 \end{bmatrix}$$

Result of RRM squaring and its row sum is

$$\begin{bmatrix} 3 & 2 & 1.8 \\ 4.5 & 3 & 2.7 \\ 5 & 3.333 & 3 \end{bmatrix} \begin{matrix} 6.8 \\ 10.2 \\ 11.3 \end{matrix}$$

The total of row sum column is 28.33. Upon normalizing row sum with total the resulting RRV is [0.24, 0.36, 0.40].

The RRM and RRV calculation of all three types of SaaS reliability metrics are the same.

6.5 Final Reliability Computation

After the completion of individual metrics value computation and priority calculation based on customer preferences, the final reliability values are calculated. Depending on the user choice, either single product reliability is provided or comparative reliability ranking of multiple products are provided.

Sample data required for metrics calculations and final reliability computation provided in this section is given in Annexure I. Readers are advised to calculate the value of each metrics and metrics priorities based on the sample preference and data provided. These calculations can be carried out with the help of Microsoft Excel. We request readers to proceed further in this section after completion of all the required computation. Most of the values used in this section are the result of the computation of previous sections of this chapter.

To calculate final reliability of a product the required values are

i. Priority of metrics of all levels.
ii. Individual metrics performance value.
iii. If multiple products are compared, then RRV value of each metrics.

If there are n levels of hierarchy in the reliability metrics, then the nth level will be atomic metrics. These are computed first. Based on these values and the priority of these metrics, $n-1$th level metrics values are computed. This goes up in the hierarchy till final reliability value is computed.

The SaaS product reliability metrics is provided as two-level hierarchy (refer Fig. 6.1). *Operational, security, support and monitoring* and *fault tolerance* are the first-level metrics which are further sub divided. We will take sub-metrics of each metrics and perform the required computation. For single product reliability the values of product P1 alone is chosen and for multiple product reliability all three products P1, P2, and P3 are used.

6.5.1 Single Product Reliability

In single product reliability calculations the priority computations and metrics performance computations are done first. Product P1 and priorities of customer C1 is chosen for sample calculation. The sub-metrics all four first-level metrics have to be calculated.

i. The values of *operational* sub-metrics are as given below.
   Workflow match (Type I) = 0.8
   Interoperability (Type I) = 0
   Migration Ease (Type II) = 0.74
   Scalability (Type II) = 0.99
   Usability (Type I) = 0.7
   Updation Frequency (Type II) = 0.7333

   The priorities of these metrics are [0.38, 0.02, 0.03, 0.14, 0.10, 0.33]. Refer Sect. 6.2 to understand the computation of the priority values. Matrix multiplication of these metrics value and the metrics priorities will result in calculation of *Operational* metric value.

$$\begin{bmatrix} 0.8 & 0 & 0.74 & 0.99 & 0.7 & 0.73 \end{bmatrix} \times \begin{bmatrix} 0.38 \\ 0.02 \\ 0.03 \\ 0.14 \\ 0.10 \\ 0.33 \end{bmatrix}$$

   The product of this is **0.776** which is the value of *operational* metrics.

ii. The values of *security* sub-metrics for product P1 are as given below

   Built-in features (Type I) = 0.873
   Security certifications (Type III) = 0.6
   Location awareness (Type II) = 0.901
   Incidence reporting (Type II) = 0.933

   The priority values of these sub-metrics are [0.45, 0.35, 0.03, 0.17]. Matrix multiplication of metric and priority values will result in the value of the *security* metric.

$$\begin{bmatrix} 0.873 & 0.6 & 0.901 & 0.933 \end{bmatrix} \times \begin{bmatrix} 0.45 \\ 0.35 \\ 0.03 \\ 0.17 \end{bmatrix}$$

The product **0.79** is the value of security metric.

iii. The values of *Support & Monitor* sub-metrics is as follows:

Compliance certificate (Type I) = 0.8
Adherence to SLA (Type II) = 0.98
Audit logs (Type II) = 0.90
Customer support (Type II) = 0.79
Notification reporting (Type II) = 0.85

The priority values of these sub-metrics are [0.17, 0.30, 0.05, 0.38, 0.10]. *Support and monitor* metric value is computed from the matrix multiplication of its sub-metrics values and priorities.

$$\begin{bmatrix} 0.8 & 0.98 & 0.90 & 0.79 & 0.85 \end{bmatrix} \times \begin{bmatrix} 0.17 \\ 0.30 \\ 0.05 \\ 0.38 \\ 0.10 \end{bmatrix}$$

The product **0.86** is the value of *Support and Monitor* sub-metric.

iv. The values of *Fault tolerance* sub-metrics is as follows:

Availability (Type II) = 0.95
Disaster management (Type I) = 0.8
Backup Frequency (Type I) = 0.82
Recovery Process (Type II) = 0.91

The priority values of these sub-metrics are [0.65, 0.05, 0.15, 0.15]. *Fault tolerance* metric value is computed from the matrix multiplication of its sub-metrics values and priorities.

$$\begin{bmatrix} 0.95 & 0.8 & 0.82 & 0.91 \end{bmatrix} \times \begin{bmatrix} 0.65 \\ 0.05 \\ 0.15 \\ 0.15 \end{bmatrix}$$

The product **0.92** is the value of *Support & Monitor* sub-metric.

After completion of computing the first-level metric values, the final reliability of the product is computed. The first-level metric priorities for customer C1 are [0.60,

0.03, 0.09, 0.28] (refer Table 6.2). The values of the first-level metrics are [0.77, 0.79, 0.86, 0.92] (refer to the above calculations). Matrix multiplication of priorities of first-level metrics with its values will provide the final reliability of the product.

$$\begin{bmatrix} 0.77\ 079\ 0.86\ 0.92 \end{bmatrix} \times \begin{bmatrix} 0.60 \\ 0.03 \\ 0.09 \\ 0.28 \end{bmatrix}$$

The result **0.824** is the final reliability of the product P1 based on the metrics preferences provided by customer C1.

6.5.2 *Reliability Based Product Ranking*

The CORE model is designed to calculate comparative reliability ranking of multiple products. RRM and RRV are used to provide the relative ranking of the product metrics value as well as the reliability value of the product. Products P1, P2, and P3 and customer preferences of C1 and C2 are used in the following computations. As mentioned at the start of Sect. 6.6.5, all sub-metric performance values has to be calculated before doing these calculations. Steps to be followed in the calculation are

1. Create RRV of all the sub-metric values.
2. Perform matrix multiplication all three products RRV of sub-metrics value with the priority of the sub-metric calculated already.
3. The final result is the relative ranking of the product based on the corresponding metric being calculated.
4. These ranking values will further be considered as the value of the first-level metrics.
5. These first-level metrics value is multiplied with its priority to compute the final reliability vector. This represents comparative ranking of the products based on reliability.

The final metrics values are mentioned in these examples with the assumption that the readers have understood the calculation of RRM and RRV (refer 6.4 for RRM and RRV calculations). Computations of the first-level metrics such as *operational, security, support and monitor* and *fault tolerance* are explained below.

i. *Operational metric*

All the sub-metric of operational metric is evaluated and listed in Table 6.14.

For each sub-metric values of all three products RRM and RRV are calculated. The RRV values of all *operational* sub-metrics are given below.

Table 6.14 Value of *operational* metrics for all three products

Sub-metric	Product (P1)	Product (P2)	Product (P3)
Work flow match	0.8	0.9	1
Interoperability	0	0	0
Migration ease	0.74	0.9828	0.881
Scalability	0.991	0.982	0.953
Usability	0.7	0.8	0.9
Updation frequency	0.733	0.775	0.822

	Work flow match	Interoperability	Migration ease	Scalability	Usability	Updation frequency
P1	0.30	0.33	0.28	0.34	0.29	0.31
P2	0.33	0.33	0.38	0.34	0.33	0.33
P3	0.37	0.33	0.34	0.33	0.38	0.35

The above matrix of RRV values has to be multiplied with the priority assigned by the customer C1 and C2 (refer Table 6.4).

The priority assigned by C1 is [0.38, 0.02, 0.03, 0.14, 0.10, 0.33] and that of customer C2 is [0.06, 0.03, 0.39, 0.11, 0.12, 0,29].

$$\begin{bmatrix} 0.30\ 0.33\ 0.28\ 0.34\ 0.29\ 0.31 \\ 0.33\ 0.33\ 0.38\ 0.34\ 0.33\ 0.33 \\ 0.37\ 0.33\ 0.34\ 0.33\ 0.38\ 0.35 \end{bmatrix} \times \begin{bmatrix} 0.38 \\ 0.02 \\ 0.03 \\ 0.14 \\ 0.10 \\ 0.33 \end{bmatrix}$$

The result product matrix with customer C1 priorities [0.30, 0.34, 0.36], which is also the relative ranking of the products based on *Operational* metric. According to customer C1 preferences the products are ranked as P3>P2>P1.

The same RRV when multiplied with the priorities assigned by customer C2 will have the resulting vector as [0.30, 0.35, 0.35]. Based on this the relative ranking is P3=P2>P1.

[0.30, 0.34, 0.36] and **[0.30, 0.35, 0.35]** is *operational* metric value of customer C1 and C2 respectively.

ii. *Security metric*

The sub-metrics values of *security* metric are listed in Table 6.15.

For each sub-metric values of all three products RRM and RRV are calculated. The RRV values of all *security* sub-metrics are given below.

Table 6.15 Sub-metrics values of *security* metric

Sub-metric	Product (P1)	Product (P2)	Product (P3)
Built-in features	0.879	0.463	0.999
Security certificates	0.6	0.8	1
Location awareness	0.901	0.953	0.956
Incidence reporting	0.933	0.9	1

	Built-in features	Security certificates	Location awareness	Incidence reporting
P1	0.375	0.240	0.32	0.33
P2	0.198	0.360	0.34	0.32
P3	0.427	0.400	0.34	0.35

The above matrix of RRV values has to be multiplied with the priority assigned by the customer C1 and C2 (refer to Table 6.6).

The priority assigned by C1 is [0.45, 0.35, 0.03, 0.17] and that of customer C2 is [0.63, 0.08, 0.25, 0.04].

$$\begin{bmatrix} 0.375 & 0.240 & 0.320 & 0.330 \\ 0.198 & 0.360 & 0.34 & 0.32 \\ 0.427 & 0.400 & 0.34 & 0.35 \end{bmatrix} \times \begin{bmatrix} 0.45 \\ 0.35 \\ 0.03 \\ 0.17 \end{bmatrix}$$

The result product matrix with customer C1 priorities [0.32, 0.28, 0.40], which is the relative ranking of the products based on *Security* metric. According to customer C1 preferences the products are ranked as P3 > P1 > P2.

The same RRV when multiplied with the priorities assigned by customer C2 will have the resulting vector as [0.35, 0.25, 0.40]. Based on this the relative ranking is P3 > P1 > P2.

[0.32, 0.28, 0.40] and **[0.35, 0.25, 0.40]** is *security* metric value of customer C1 and C2 respectively.

iii. *Support and monitor metric*

The sub-metrics values of *support and monitor* metric are listed in Table 6.16.

For each sub-metric values of all three products RRM and RRV are calculated. The RRV values of all *support and monitor* sub-metrics are given below.

Table 6.16 *Support and monitor* sub-metric values

Sub-metric	Product (P1)	Product (P2)	Product (P3)
Compliance certificates	0.8	0.6	1
Adherence to SLA	0.983	0.996	0.999
Audit logs	0.908	0.784	0.995
Support	0.795	0.863	0.934
Notification reports	0.85	0.785	0.88

	Compliance certificates	Adherence to SLA	Audit logs	Support	Notification reports
P1	0.33	0.33	0.34	0.31	0.34
P2	0.25	0.33	0.29	0.33	0.31
P3	0.42	0.34	0.37	0.36	0.35

The above matrix of RRV values has to be multiplied with the priority assigned by the customer C1 and C2 (refer to Table 6.8).

The priority assigned by C1 is [0.17, 0.30, 0.05, 0.38, 0.10] and that of customer C2 is [0.14, 0.44, 0.04, 0.32, 0.06].

$$\begin{bmatrix} 0.33\ 0.33\ 0.34\ 0.31\ 0.34 \\ 0.25\ 0.33\ 0.29\ 0.33\ 0.31 \\ 0.42\ 0.34\ 0.37\ 0.36\ 0.35 \end{bmatrix} \times \begin{bmatrix} 0.17 \\ 0.30 \\ 0.05 \\ 0.38 \\ 0.10 \end{bmatrix}$$

The result product matrix with customer C1 priorities [0.32, 0.32, 0.36], which is the relative ranking of the products based on *support and monitor* metric. According to customer C1 preferences the products are ranked as P3 > P1 = P2.

The same RRV when multiplied with the priorities assigned by customer C2 will have the resulting vector as [0.32, 0.32, 0.36]. Based on this the relative ranking is P3 > P1 = P2.

[0.32, 0.32, 0.36] and **[0.32, 0.32, 0.36]** is *support and monitor* metric value of customer C1 and C2 respectively.

iv. *Fault tolerance metric*

The sub-metrics values of *fault tolerance* metric are listed in Table 6.17.

For each sub-metric values of all three products RRM and RRV are calculated. The RRV values of all *fault tolerance* sub-metrics are given below.

Table 6.17 *Fault tolerance* sub-metric values

Sub-metric	Product (P1)	Product (P2)	Product (P3)
Availability	0.96	0.99	0.999
Disaster management	0.8	0.7	0.9
Backup frequency	0.827	0.911	0.999
Recovery time	0.912	0.975	0.987

	Availability	Disaster management	Backup frequency	Recovery time
P1	0.32	0.33	0.30	0.32
P2	0.34	0.29	0.33	0.34
P3	0.34	0.38	0.37	0.34

The above matrix of RRV values has to be multiplied with the priority assigned by the customer C1 and C2 (refer to Table 6.10).

The priority assigned by C1 is [0.65, 0.05, 0.15, 0.15] and that of customer C2 is [0.73, 0.09, 0.09, 0.09].

$$\begin{bmatrix} 0.32 & 0.33 & 0.30 & 0.32 \\ 0.34 & 0.29 & 0.33 & 0.34 \\ 0.34 & 0.38 & 0.37 & 0.34 \end{bmatrix} \times \begin{bmatrix} 0.65 \\ 0.05 \\ 0.15 \\ 0.15 \end{bmatrix}$$

The result product matrix with customer C1 priorities [0.32, 0.33, 0.35], which is the relative ranking of the products based on *Fault tolerance* metric. According to customer C1 preferences the products are ranked as P3 > P2 > P1.

The same RRV when multiplied with the priorities assigned by customer C2 will have the resulting vector as [0.32, 0.33, 0.35]. Based on this the relative ranking is P3 > P2 > P1.

[0.32, 0.33, 0.35] and **[0.32, 0.33, 0.35]** is *fault tolerance* metric value of customer C1 and C2 respectively.

After completion of metric value calculation for all the first-level metrics, the priorities of these are used to compute final comparative reliability ranking of the products. The priority of the first-level metrics of customer C1 is [0.60, 0.03, 0.09, 0.28] and that of customer C2 is [0.19, 0.68, 0.09, 0.04] (refer Table 6.2).

Reliability ranking based on customer C1 priority assignment is given below. There are four first-level metrics and three products are being compared. Hence 3 × 4 matrix is used.

$$\begin{bmatrix} 0.30 & 0.32 & 0.32 & 0.32 \\ 0.34 & 0.28 & 0.33 & 0.33 \\ 0.36 & 0.40 & 0.36 & 0.35 \end{bmatrix} \times \begin{bmatrix} 0.60 \\ 0.03 \\ 0.09 \\ 0.28 \end{bmatrix}$$

The resulting product vector is [0.31, 0.33, 0.36]. This also provides ranking of the products as P3 > P2 > P1. This ranking is as per customer C1 preferences.

Reliability ranking based on customer C1 priority assignment is given below.

$$\begin{bmatrix} 0.30 & 0.35 & 0.32 & 0.32 \\ 0.35 & 0.25 & 0.33 & 0.33 \\ 0.35 & 0.40 & 0.36 & 0.35 \end{bmatrix} \times \begin{bmatrix} 0.19 \\ 0.68 \\ 0.09 \\ 0.04 \end{bmatrix}$$

The resulting product vector is [0.34, 0.28, 0.38]. This also provides ranking of the products as P3 > P1 > P2. This ranking is as per customer C2 preferences.

The variation in the same set of product ranking based on the user preferences is a proof that the model is customer-oriented model.

6.6 Summary

This chapter deals with the complete numerical calculations used in the CORE model. For easy understanding sample preferences from two different customers C1 and C2 are accepted. These two customers have varying business needs but are willing to adopt cloud application for accounting purposes. Three different products chosen are named as P1, P2, and P3 to maintain anonymity. Preference acceptance of all the metrics and sub-metrics along with its priority calculations for both customers is explained. The metrics performance calculations are discussed in detail with the help of sample data. Separate examples are discussed for three type of metrics calculations such as type I, type II, and type III. Relative Reliability Matrix and Relative Reliability Vector calculations discussed with example of a metric. The last section of the chapter explains computation of reliability for a single product and also for a group of products. Readers are advised to proceed for the last section after attempting metric performance calculations based on the ample data provided in annexure 1.

Reference

BPMSG. (2017). *AHP—High Consistency Ratio*. Retrieved June 2018 from https://bpmsg.com/ahp-high-consistency-ratio/.

Annexure
Sample Data for SaaS Reliability Calculations

SaaS reliability metrics is categorized into levels and priority of reliability metrics, needs to be assigned for final reliability evaluation. Sample data for priority and individual metrics is provided in this annexure to demonstrate the calculations.

Note

Table A.1, A.2, A.3, A.4 and A.5 provides comparitive metric preferences for all levels of reliability metrics. In Table A.1 some of the metric preference value is given as "–". For example metric preference between *operational* and *security* is provided as 8 but metric preference between *security* and *operational* is given as "–". This is because if we provide preference say *p* between metric *M1* and *M2*, then preference between *M2* and *M1* is calculated as *1/p*. Hence forth in the succeeding tables only value preferences are provided the reciprocals have to be assumed during calculation.

Based on the above data the preference values can be calculated and the final values are given in Fig. A.1.

Sample data for individual metrics for SaaS reliability calculation is given below. These can be used for practicing reliability calculation. Three product details are given using which either single product reliability or reliability based comparative ranking can be calculated. Three products are named as P1, P2, and P3. Only sample data and various calculation headings are given. Readers are encouraged to do the calculations

1. *Workflow match (Type I metric)*

   Total functionality requirement of the customer is 10
   P1 matches 8 functionalities
   P2 matches 9 functionalities
   P3 matches 10 functionalities

V. Kumar and R. Vidhyalakshmi, *Reliability Aspect of Cloud Computing Environment*, https://doi.org/10.1007/978-981-13-3023-0

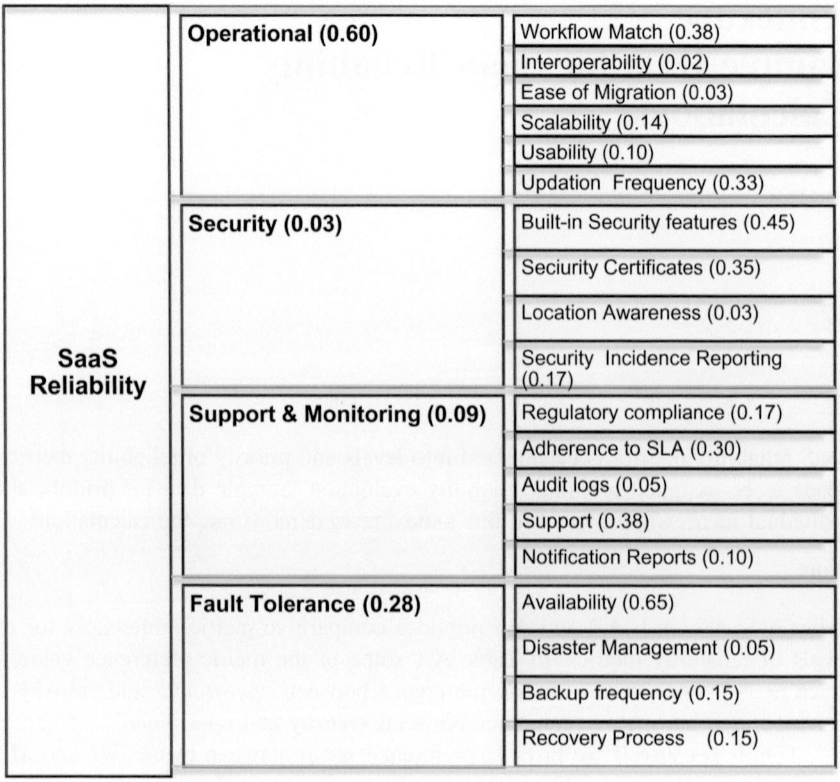

Fig. A.1 Computed preferences for SaaS reliability metric

Table A.1 Comparative preferences for first level metrics

First-level metric	Preference	First-level metrics
Operational	8	Security
	5	Support and monitoring
	5	Fault tolerance
Security	–	Operational
	–	Support and monitoring
		Fault tolerance
Support and monitoring	–	Operational
	5	Security
	–	Fault tolerance
Fault tolerance	–	Operational
	7	Security
	5	Support and monitoring

Table A.2 Comparative preferences for *Operational* metric

Operational sub-metrics	Metrics preference	*Operational* sub-metrics
Work flow match	9	Interoperability
	8	Migration ease
	7	Scalability
	5	Usability
	4	Updation frequency
Migration ease	4	Interoperability
Scalability	8	Interoperability
	5	Migration ease
	3	Usability
Usability	5	Interoperability
	7	Migration ease
Updation frequency	9	Interoperability
	7	Migration ease
	5	Scalability
	5	Usability

Table A.3 Comparative preferences for *Security* sub-metric

Security sub-metrics	Metrics preference	*Security* sub-metrics
Built-in features	5	Certificates
	9	Location awareness
	1	Incidence reporting
Certificates	7	Location awareness
	5	Incidence reporting
Incidence reporting	9	Location awareness

Table A.4 Comparative preferences for *Support and Monitor* sub-metrics

Support and Monitor sub-metrics	Metrics preference	*Support and Monitor* sub-metrics
Compliance report	3	Audit logs
	3	Notification report
Adherence to SLA	3	Compliance report
	5	Audit logs
	3	Notification report
Customer support	3	Compliance report
	2	Adherence to SLA
	4	Audit logs
	3	Notification report
Notification report	3	Audit logs

Table A.5 Comparative preferences of *Fault tolerance* sub-metrics

Fault tolerance sub-metrics	Metrics preference	*Fault tolerance* sub-metrics
Availability	9	Disaster management
	5	Backup frequency
	5	Recovery time
Backup frequency	3	Disaster management
	1	Recovery time
Recovery time	3	Disaster management
	1	Backup frequency

2. *Interoperability (Type I metric)*

If the organization is involving cloud applications without any previous software setup, then this metric will have 0 as its value for all the products. If any previous in-house application exists that needs to be ported onto cloud application setup, then input will be

Total number of modules to be ported 10
P1 can port 8 modules within minimum specified time
P2 can port 7 modules within minimum specified time
P3 can port 10 modules within minimum specified time

3. *Migration ease (Type II metric) chi-square method*

obs	assu	$(\text{obs} - \text{assu})^2/\text{assu}$	obs	assu	$(\text{obs} - \text{assu})^2/\text{assu}$	obs	assu	$(\text{obs} - \text{ssu})^2/\text{assu}$
20	20		43	40		35	35	
21	20		40	40		35	35	
25	20		41	40		36	35	
20	20		45	40		35	35	
22	20		46	40		37	35	
28	20		40	40		45	35	
23	20		43	40		40	35	
24	20		44	40		38	35	
20	20		40	40		35	35	
20	20		41	40		39	35	
Total			Total			Total		

Probability Q value of χ^2 has to be calculated with degree of freedom as 9 as 10 customer values are given in the table. χ^2 calculator link https://www.fourmilab.ch/rpkp/experiments/analysis/chiCalc.html.

4. *Scalability (Type II metric) binomial distribution method*

No. of scale	Success scale	Prob	No. of scale	Success scale	Prob	No. of scale	Success scale	Prob
5	4		5	5		9	8	
7	7		9	6		10	10	
9	8		9	9		10	7	
10	8		10	10		10	8	
5	5		6	6		10	6	
5	4		5	5		9	8	
7	7		9	6		10	10	
9	8		9	9		10	7	
10	8		10	10		10	8	
5	5		6	6		10	6	
Average			Average			Average		

5. *Usability (Type I metric)*

Total number of usable features required = 10
Product P1 has satisfied 7 usable features
Product P2 satisfies 8 usable features
Product P3 satisfies 9 usable features

6. *Updation frequency (Type II method) chi-square method*

obs	assu	$(obs - assu)^2/assu$	obs	assu	$(obs - assu)^2/assu$	obs	assu	$(obs - assu)^2/assu$
6	6		10	12		8	9	
3	6		9	12		7	9	
4	6		8	12		6	9	
6	6		11	12		5	9	
5	6		12	12		9	9	
4	6		10	12		6	9	
3	6		8	12		7	9	
2	6		9	12		8	9	
6	6		7	12		9	9	
5	6		9	12		9	9	

7. *Built-in features (Type II and Type III metric)*

Step 1: Calculation for the presence of built-in features
Total built-in features required = 10
Present in product P1 = 9
Present in product P2 = 8
Present in product P3 = 10
Step 2: Assurance of the feature presence

obs	assu	$(obs - assu)^2/assu$	obs	assu	$(obs - assu)^2/assu$	obs	assu	$(obs - assu)^2/assu$
7	9		5	8		9	10	
9	9		6	8		10	10	
8	9		7	8		9	10	
7	9		6	8		9	10	
6	9		7	8		9	10	
7	9		5	8		10	10	
8	9		5	8		10	10	
9	9		6	8		10	10	
9	9		5	8		10	10	
9	9		6	8		10	10	
Total			Total			Total		

Average of step 1 and step 2 is taken as final value

8. *Security certificates (Type I method)*

Total certificates required = 10
Product P1 has 6 certificates
P2 has 8 certificates and P3 has 10 certificates

9. *Location awareness (Type II metric) simple division method*

DC	TM	Eff (DC/TM)	DC	TM	Eff (DC/TM)	DC	TM	Eff (DC/TM)
7	9		9	9		6	6	
5	5		8	8		7	7	
9	10		5	5		5	6	
4	4		6	6		6	6	
7	8		6	7		5	5	
9	12		8	8		6	6	
5	7		5	5		6	7	
6	6		7	9		7	8	
7	7		8	8		7	7	
3	3		9	10		6	6	
Average			Average			Average		

In the above table DC is the data movement to the correct location and TM is the total number of data movements.

10. *Incidence reporting (Type II metric) simple division method*

NI	TI	Eff (NI/TI)	NI	TI	Eff (NI/TI)	NI	TI	Eff (NI/TI)
3	3		2	2		3	3	
2	3		2	2		3	3	
3	3		1	2		3	3	
3	3		2	2		3	3	
3	3		2	2		3	3	
3	3		2	2		3	3	
3	3		1	2		3	3	
2	3		2	2		3	3	
3	3		2	2		3	3	
3	3		2	2		3	3	
Average			Average			Average		

In the above table NI is the number of incidences that were reported to customers and TI is the total number of security incidences.

11. *Regulatory compliance certificates (Type III metric)*

Total certificates required = 10
Product P1 has 8 certificates
P2 has 6 certificates and P3 has 10 certificates

12. *Adherence to SLA (Type II metric) chi-square test*

obs	assu	$(obs - assu)^2/assu$	obs	assu	$(obs - assu)^2/assu$	obs	assu	$(obs - assu)^2/assu$
9	10		8	10		9	10	
8	10		8	10		9	10	
9	10		8	10		9	10	
8	10		9	10		9	10	
10	10		9	10		9	10	
7	10		9	10		10	10	
8	10		9	10		10	10	
9	10		10	10		10	10	
10	10		10	10		10	10	
10	10		10	10		10	10	
Total			Total			Total		

13. *Audit logs (Type II metric) binomial distribution method*

Step 1: Successful log access
Total number of customers surveyed = 10
Number of successful for P1 = 8; P2 = 7; P3 = 9
Probability of successful access P1, P2 and P3 to be calculated

Step 2: Successful log retention
Total number of customers surveyed = 10
Number of successful for P1 = 6; P2 = 5; P3 = 10
Probability of successful access P1, P2 and P3 to be calculated
Average for the above two values have to be calculated for P1, P2 and P3.

14. *Support (Type II metric) simple division method*

Step 1: Support hour reliability

CC	TC	Eff (CC/TC)	CC	TC	Eff (CC/TC)	CC	TC	Eff (CC/TC)
9	12		9	10		9	9	
5	15		8	9		6	6	
7	8		6	9		7	8	
10	10		8	9		7	7	
7	10		12	15		9	9	
8	12		10	10		7	7	
5	9		5	6		5	6	
4	5		7	7		7	8	
9	15		8	9		7	7	
8	8		8	8		8	8	
Average			Average			Average		

In the above table CC is the number of call connected and TC is the total number of calls made.

Step 2: Response time reliability

RWT	TR	Eff (RWT/TR)	RWT	TR	Eff (RWT/TR)	RWT	TR	Eff (RWT/TR)
6	8		8	9		7	7	
8	10		7	9		5	6	
5	5		6	7		6	6	
7	8		8	9		5	6	
7	10		10	12		9	9	
6	7		6	8		7	7	
8	8		6	6		4	5	
4	5		7	7		5	8	

(continued)

(continued)

RWT	TR	Eff (RWT/TR)	RWT	TR	Eff (RWT/TR)	RWT	TR	Eff (RWT/TR)
9	12		7	9		7	7	
7	8		5	6		8	8	
Average			Average			Average		

In the above table RWT is the number of responses within time and TR is the total number of responses.

Step 3: Resolution time reliability

SWT	TS	Eff (SWT/TS)	SWT	TS	Eff (SWT/TS)	SWT	TS	Eff (SWT/TS)
5	8		9	9		7	7	
8	10		6	9		6	6	
4	5		6	7		6	6	
8	8		8	9		5	6	
6	10		9	12		8	9	
5	7		6	8		7	7	
8	8		5	6		5	5	
4	5		6	7		5	8	
10	12		9	9		7	7	
8	8		5	6		8	8	
Average			Average			Average		

In the above table SWT is the number of solutions provided within assured time and TS is the total number of solutions provided.

Average value of step 1, 2, and 3 will be the final value of *support* metric

15. *Notification report (Type II metric) simple division method*

NC	TC	Eff (NC/TC)	NC	TC	Eff (NC/TC)	NC	TC	Eff (NC/TC)
9	10		7	7		5	5	
10	10		6	7		4	5	
7	10		5	7		5	5	
6	10		6	7		5	5	
7	10		5	7		4	5	
8	10		4	7		3	5	
9	10		7	7		5	5	
10	10		6	7		5	5	
10	10		5	7		3	5	
9	10		4	7		5	5	
Average			Average			Average		

In the above table NC is the number of notification received by the customer TC is the total number of changes that had happened in the Service agreement.

16. *Availability (Type II metric) chi-square method*

The availability hours is calculated for a month. Total number of service availability hours = 30 * 24 = 720. Based on the availability assurance the expected availability hours is calculated. For example if the availability assured if 95%, then 95% * 720 will be the expected hours.

obs	Assu (95%)	$(obs - assu)^2$/ assu	obs	Assu (99.9%)	$(obs - assu)^2$/ assu	obs	Assu (99.99%)	$(obs - assu)^2$ /assu
680	684		700	712.8		710	719.28	
678	684		698	712.8		705	719.28	
664	684		710	712.8		719	719.28	
650	684		703	712.8		715	719.28	
679	684		705	712.8		719	719.28	
683	684		700	712.8		716	719.28	
680	684		712	712.8		719	719.28	
679	684		701	712.8		715	719.28	
662	684		700	712.8		719	719.28	
684	684		705	712.8		719	719.28	
Total			Total			Total		

17. *Disaster management (Type I metric)*

Total number of DR features required by customer = 10
Number of DR features present in P1 = 8; P2 = 7; P3 = 9

18. *Backup frequency (Type II metric) chi-square method)*

This metric is calculated as average of three values such as mirroring latency, adherence to assured backup frequency and backup retention capacity.

Step 1: Mirroring latency (measured in minutes)

obs	Assu	$(obs - assu)^2$/ assu	obs	Assu	$(obs - assu)^2$ / assu	obs	Assu	$(obs - assu)^2$/ assu
6	5		7	5		5	5	
7	5		6	5		6	5	
5	5		8	5		5	5	
7	5		6	5		5	5	
8	5		7	5		5	5	
5	5		8	5		5	5	
6	5		5	5		5	5	
7	5		5	5		6	5	
8	5		5	5		6	5	
7	5		6	5		5	5	
Total			Total			Total		

Step 2: Backup frequency (measured a number of backups taken in a month)

obs	Assu	(obs − assu)^2/ assu	obs	Assu	(obs − assu)^2/ assu	obs	Assu	(obs − assu)^2/ assu
9	10		10	12		15	15	
7	10		11	12		15	15	
7	10		12	12		14	15	
9	10		11	12		13	15	
10	10		9	12		15	15	
7	10		12	12		15	15	
7	10		11	12		15	15	
8	10		10	12		14	15	
8	10		9	12		15	15	
10	10		11	12		14	15	
Total			Total			Total		

Step 3: Backup retention (measured in terms of number of days)

Obs	Assu	(obs − assu)^2/ assu	obs	Assu	(obs − assu)^2/ assu	obs	Assu	(obs − assu)^2/ assu
28	30		19	20		35	35	
30	30		18	20		34	35	
30	30		20	20		35	35	
29	30		20	20		35	35	
30	30		19	20		35	35	
27	30		18	20		35	35	
30	30		20	20		34	35	
26	30		25	20		33	35	
30	30		20	20		35	35	
29	30		19	20		35	35	
Total			Total			Total		

19. *Recovery process (Type II metric) binomial distribution method*

NR	NSR	Prob	NR	NSR	Prob	NR	NSR	Prob
5	5		4	3		3	3	
5	4		4	4		3	3	
5	3		4	3		3	3	
5	4		4	4		3	3	
5	5		4	3		3	3	
5	3		4	4		3	3	

(continued)

(continued)

NR	NSR	Prob	NR	NSR	Prob	NR	NSR	Prob
5	3		4	4		3	3	
5	4		4	4		3	3	
5	3		4	4		3	2	
5	4		4	3		3	3	
Average			Average			Average		

In the above table NR represents total number of recovery processes attempted and NSR represents total number of successful recovery processes.

MIX
Papier aus verantwortungsvollen Quellen
Paper from responsible sources
FSC® C105338

If you have any concerns about our products,
you can contact us on
ProductSafety@springernature.com

In case Publisher is established outside the EU,
the EU authorized representative is:
Springer Nature Customer Service Center GmbH
Europaplatz 3, 69115 Heidelberg, Germany

Printed by Libri Plureos GmbH
in Hamburg, Germany